Higher
Geography
Practice Papers for SQA Exams

Sheena Williamson

Contents

HODDER
GIBSON
AN HACHETTE UK COMPANY

The Publishers would like to thank the following for permission to reproduce copyright material:

Exam rubrics at the start of Section 1, Section 2 and Section 3 of each practice paper are reproduced by kind permission of SQA, Copyright © Scottish Qualifications Authority.

Ordnance Survey maps on pages 16–17, 38–9, 58–9, 62 are reproduced by permission of Ordnance Survey on behalf of HMSO. © Crown copyright 2017. All rights reserved. Ordnance Survey Licence number 100047450.

Photo credits: p.5 © Phil MacD Photography/Shutterstock; p.11 © Bill Bachmann/Alamy Stock Photo; p.18 © Dave Ellison/Alamy Stock Photo; p.28 (l) © Joerg Boethling/Alamy Stock Photo, (r) © Ariadne Van Zandbergen/Alamy Stock Photo; p.29 © delcreations/123RF; p.34 © Heather Snow/123RF; p.48 (tl) © Rosaline Napier/Shutterstock, (tr) © Tosca Weijers/Shutterstock, (bl) © ALAN OLIVER/Alamy Stock Photo, (br) © George Robertson/Shutterstock; p.51 © Jeremy Sutton-Hibbert/Alamy Stock Photo; p.53 (b) © Planetphoto.ch/Shutterstock; p.63 © Joe Gough/Shutterstock.

Acknowledgements: p.7 Diagram Q4, *Daily Pakistan Global*, 15/6/16; p.8, © United Nations Convention to Combat Desertification (UNCCD); p.12 © TnT Designs/Shutterstock; p.13 Diagram Q9, © *Daily Record*, 12/1/17; p.15 Diagram Q11A, adapted from DECC; Diagram Q11B, © *Our Choice*, 2009; p.19 Diagram Q12D, adapted from www.ukhillwalking.com, Diagram Q12E, adapted from www.quarrybattery.com; p.26 Question 3, adapted from SQA Higher Geography past paper 2016, Copyright © Scottish Qualifications Authority; p.40 Diagram Q12, adapted from www.gov.scot; p.42 Diagram Q12C, from Balmaha Biodiversity Community Action (BBCA) press release; Diagram Q12D, © James Fraser, Chairman, Friends of Loch Lomond and The Trossachs; p.49 Diagram Q4, adapted from www.fdbetancor.com; p.53 Diagram Q7A, adapted from SQA Intermediate 2 Paper 2013, Copyright © Scottish Qualifications Authority; p.56 Diagram Q10, adapted from www.economist.com; p.57 Diagram Q11B, adapted from www.iea.org; p.60 Diagram Q12A, adapted from www.hebwx.co.uk; p.61 Diagram Q12B (logo and text), RSPB website © RSPB; p.64 Diagram Q12F (text and tl logo), www.stornowaywind.co.uk © Stornoway Wind Farm.

Every effort has been made to trace all copyright holders, but if any have been inadvertently overlooked the Publishers will be pleased to make the necessary arrangements at the first opportunity.

Orders: please contact Bookpoint Ltd, 130 Park Drive, Milton Park, Abingdon, Oxon OX14 4SE. Telephone: (44) 01235 827720. Fax: (44) 01235 400454. Lines are open 9.00–5.00, Monday to Saturday, with a 24-hour message answering service. Visit our website at www.hoddereducation.co.uk. Hodder Gibson can be contacted direct on: Tel: 0141 333 4650; Fax: 0141 404 8188; email: hoddergibson@hodder.co.uk

© Sheena Williamson 2017

First published in 2017 by
Hodder Gibson, an imprint of Hodder Education,
An Hachette UK Company
211 St Vincent Street
Glasgow G2 5QY

Impression number   5 4 3 2 1
Year   2021 2020 2019 2018 2017

Cover photo © Lightwise/123RF.com
Illustrations by Aptara, Inc.
Typeset in Din regular 12/14.4 pt by Aptara Inc.
Printed in the UK

A catalogue record for this title is available from the British Library

ISBN: 978 1 5104 1508 9

Introduction

Higher Geography

Layout of the book

This book contains model papers which reflect the actual SQA exam as much as possible. The layout of each paper, the types of question and the mark allocation are similar to the actual exam that you will sit so you will become familiar with what the exam paper will look like. Each model paper has detailed answers for each question. Marks within an answer are indicated by **(1)**. This allows you to see where marks are gained as well the amount of detail required for a point.

Each answer has a hint attached. These give you practical tips on how to answer certain types of question, some common errors when answering questions and advice on how to gain maximum marks from your answers. The book also contains a revision grid. This grid shows you the topics/questions covered in the model papers. This allows you to easily find a particular topic or question you want to revise.

For further information on the assignment and the course content and notes, you should refer to Hodder Gibson's SQA-endorsed Higher textbook and *How to Pass* Higher Geography book. Used in conjunction with these practice papers they should give you the best opportunity to achieve the best result for the course. Cross-references to the *HTP* book are supplied in the student margin.

Course assessment

The course assessment will consist of two parts: a question paper (60 marks) and an assignment (30 marks). The question paper is therefore worth two thirds of the overall marks of the course assessment, and the assignment one third.

The assignment is completed throughout the year and submitted to SQA to be marked around April. This is worth 30 marks. These marks are then added to the marks achieved in the exam paper to give you a final award.

The question paper

The purpose of the question paper is to allow you to demonstrate the skills you have acquired and to reveal the knowledge and understanding you have gained from the topics studied throughout the course. The question paper will give you the chance to show your ability in interpreting, explaining, evaluating and analysing a wide range of geographical information as well as using a wide range of maps and demonstrating competence in Ordnance Survey (OS) skills. Candidates will complete this question paper in 2 hours and 15 minutes. Questions will be asked on a local, regional and global scale. The question paper has four sections.

Section 1: Physical Environments is worth 15 marks. Candidates will answer all questions in this section. These are made up of extended response questions. Your answers should demonstrate knowledge and understanding of the processes and interactions taking place within physical environments on a local, regional and global scale. The topics you can be asked questions on include: Atmosphere, for example Intertropical Convergence Zone (ITCZ), global heat budget, atmospheric and oceanic circulation; Hydrosphere, for example hydrographs, hydrological cycle; Lithosphere, for example glaciated and coastal features, land use conflicts and management; and Biosphere, for example soils.

Section 2: Human Environments is worth 15 marks. Candidates will answer all questions in this section. These are made up of extended response questions. Your answers should demonstrate knowledge and understanding of the processes and interactions taking place within urban and rural environments in both developed and developing countries. The topics you can be asked questions on include: Population, for example census, population structure and migration; Rural, for example impact and management of rural land degradation on a rainforest or semi-arid area; and Urban, for example recent changes in housing and transport, and management and impact of these changes.

Section 3: Global Issues is worth 20 marks (two questions, each worth 10 marks). In this section you have a choice of extended response questions. Candidates will answer two questions from a choice of five. Your answers should demonstrate knowledge and understanding of global issues as well as evaluating strategies used to manage issues. You should have an understanding of the need for sustainable development. Topics include: River Basin Management; Development and Health; Global Climate Change; Trade, Aid and Geopolitics; and Energy.

Section 4: Application of Geographical Skills – Scenario. The scenario question is worth 10 marks. It is designed to examine your geographical skills. This type of question builds on the skills you acquired at National 5. These skills include interpreting an Ordnance Survey map, using six-figure grid references, understanding/using scale, direction and distance. You should also be able to extract and interpret information from a variety of graphs and charts, for example bar graphs, line graphs, pie charts, climate graphs, etc. In this question you will be able to demonstrate to the examiner the geographical skills you have learned and developed throughout your Higher course. You will be given a variety of resources to use and make judgements on, including an Ordnance Survey map and other resources. You will also be given a set of conditions to follow. These should be used to help you answer the question. You should use/evaluate the information you have been given to make judgements and back up your answer with map evidence, information from the diagrams, etc. Remember, the diagrams and OS map are there for a purpose and contain valuable information that you should incorporate in your answer!

More detailed information on these topics can be found on the SQA Geography website at www.sqa.org.uk.

Choices

In the Physical Environments and Human Environments sections there are no choice questions. All questions need to be answered. However, the topics asked in each section can vary from year to year – for example in the Physical Environments section there could be questions from the Biosphere, the Hydrosphere and the Lithosphere topics and none from the Atmosphere topic, but the following year the topics could change. The same is true for the Human Environments section. In the Global Issues section there is a choice. You need to complete **only two** questions. If you answer all five questions you will not have enough time to put in the detail needed to gain full marks for the two questions required.

Common errors

Lack of sufficient detail

Many candidates fail to provide sufficient detail in answers, often by omitting reference to specific examples, elaborating or developing points made in their answer. Remember, much more information is needed in your answers than at National 5 to gain a mark. The more detail, the more marks. If asked for a named example and you do not provide one, you will lose marks. If the question specifically asks for a diagram, again you will lose marks if you do not include one in your answer. If you are asked to explain and you simply describe, you will score limited marks.

Irrelevant answers

You must read the question instructions carefully to avoid giving answers which are irrelevant to the question. If you go off at a tangent you will use up valuable time that could have been used to complete the paper. Be careful with questions like those found in the Urban section, which can relate to either a developing or a developed country.

Repetition

You should be careful not to repeat points already made in your answer. These will not gain any further marks. You may feel that you have written a long answer, but it may contain the same basic information repeated over and over. Unfortunately, these statements will be recognised and ignored when your paper is marked.

Listing/bullet points

If you give a simple list of points rather than fuller statements in your answer you may lose marks, for example in a 5-mark question you will obtain only 1 mark for a list. The same rule applies to a simple list of bullet points.

Statement reversals

Occasionally questions involve opposites. For example, some answers would say 'Death rates are high in developing countries due to poor health care' and then go on to say 'Death rates are low in developed countries due to good health care'. Avoid doing this. You are simply stating the reverse of the first statement. A better second statement might be that 'High standards of hygiene, health and education in developed countries have helped to bring about low death rates'.

Types of question and command words

In these model papers, and in the exam itself, a number of command words will be used in the different types of question you will encounter. The command words are used to show you how you should answer a question – some words indicate that you should write more than others. If you familiarise yourself with these command words, it will help you to structure your answers more effectively. The question types to look out for are listed below.

Explain

These questions ask you to explain, meaning you have to give reasons in your answer. If resources are provided in the question, make sure you refer to them in your answer. Some marks may be allowed for description but these will be quite restricted. Command words may include: analyse; evaluate; discuss.

Analyse

This involves identifying parts and the relationships between them by showing links between different components, linking components and related concepts, noting similarities and differences, explaining possible consequences and implications, explaining the impact of, for example, processes of degradation, or strategies adopted to control events, or government policies on people and the environment.

Evaluate

This will involve making judgements on the relative success or failure of strategies and projects such as a river basin management scheme or aid programme.

Discuss

These questions ask you to develop your thoughts on a specific project, or change in specified situations. You may be asked to consider both sides of an argument and provide a range of comments on the arguments.

The exam

Duration: 2 hours, 15 minutes

Total marks: 60

Section 1	Physical Environments	15 marks
Section 2	Human Environments	15 marks
Section 3	Global Issues	20 marks (answer two 10-mark questions)
Section 4	Scenario	10 marks

Section 1

Attempt all questions.

Section 2

Attempt all questions.

Section 3

Answer two questions from five.

Section 4

Attempt question.

Time management is important. The exam lasts for 135 minutes. This means you have about 20 minutes to answer a 10-mark question and about 30 minutes to answer a 15-mark question. This allows you 15 minutes to read through the question paper at the beginning and check your paper at the end.

Remember: Read the instructions carefully. Read the questions carefully. Answer in as much detail as possible.

Good luck!

Higher Geography

Revision grid

	Paper A	Paper B	Paper C
PHYSICAL ENVIRONMENTS			
Atmosphere – energy surplus	Q1		
Atmosphere – ITCZ		Q3	
Lithosphere – coasts – formation of sand spit	Q2		
Lithosphere – upland glaciation – formation of corrie			Q2
Lithosphere – lowland glaciation – formation of terminal moraine, drumlin or esker		Q2	
Lithosphere – land use conflicts			Q3
Hydrosphere – hydrological cycle	Q3		
Hydrosphere – factors affecting a hydrograph		Q1	
Biosphere – soil formation			Q1
HUMAN ENVIRONMENTS			
Population – census	Q4		
Population – population structure			Q4
Population – impact of migration on receiving country		Q4	
Rural – impact of degradation	Q5		
Rural – effectiveness of strategies to reduce land degradation			Q5
Rural – strategies used to manage rural land degradation		Q5	
Urban – traffic management strategies – developed	Q6		
Urban – housing management – developed			Q6
Urban – strategies to improve shanty towns		Q6	
GLOBAL ISSUES			
River Basin Management			
Physical and human factors affecting the site of a dam	Q7a		
Evaluate three dam sites			Q7a
Negative environmental impacts of a major dam	Q7b		
Evaluation of environmental impacts			Q7b
Need for water management		Q7a	
Positive impact of water management		Q7b	
Development and Health			
Primary health care strategies	Q8a		
Effectiveness of strategies	Q8b		
Development indictors			Q8a
Reasons for differences in development			Q8b
Combat of disease – malaria, cholera or bilharzia		Q8a	
Evaluation of success of measures to combat disease		Q8b	

	Paper A	Paper B	Paper C
Global Climate Change			
Human causes of global climate change	Q9a		
Physical causes of global climate change			Q9a
Consequences on local and national scale	Q9b		
Global effects of climate change			Q9b
Reducing global warming		Q9a	
Effectiveness of strategies to reduce global warming		Q9b	
Trade, Aid and Geopolitics			
Inequalities in trade	Q10a		
Impact of inequalities on developed and developing countries	Q10b		
Impact of economic changes on developing countries			Q10a
Fair trade			Q10b
Impact of unfair trade on developing countries		Q10a	
Strategies to reduce inequalities in world trade		Q10b	
Energy			
Changes in energy production	Q11a		
Generating energy from renewable resources	Q11b		
Effectiveness of non-renewable energy sources			Q11a
Growth in energy demand			Q11b
Reasons for increased energy consumption		Q11a	
Advantages of renewables meeting energy demand		Q11b	
OS/Scenarios			
Llanberis proposed HEP scheme	Q12		
Balmaha proposed housing development			Q12
Stornoway proposed wind farm		Q12	

Higher
Geography

Duration: 2 hours and 15 minutes

Total marks: 60

Section 1 – PHYSICAL ENVIRONMENTS – 15 MARKS

Attempt ALL questions.

Section 2 – HUMAN ENVIRONMENTS – 15 MARKS

Attempt ALL questions.

Section 3 – GLOBAL ISSUES – 20 MARKS

Attempt TWO questions.

Section 4 – APPLICATION OF GEOGRAPHICAL SKILLS – 10 MARKS

Attempt the question.

Credit will be given for appropriately labelled sketch maps and diagrams.

Write your answers clearly in the spaces provided in this paper. You must clearly identify the question number you are attempting.

Use **blue** or **black** ink.

A

Section 1: Physical Environments

Total marks: 15

Attempt ALL questions.

	MARKS	STUDENT MARGIN
Question 1 Explain why there is a surplus of solar energy in tropical latitudes and a deficit of solar energy towards the poles. You may wish to use a diagram(s) in your answer.	5	HTP Page 2/3

MARKS STUDENT MARGIN

Question 2

Diagram Q2: Spurn Head Spit, UK

Look at Diagram Q2, which shows Spurn Head Spit in the UK.

Explain, with the aid of a diagram(s), the processes involved in the formation of a sand spit.

5

HTP
Page 23

A

STUDENT
MARKS | MARGIN

Question 3 Discuss ways in which human activity can affect the hydrological cycle.

5 | HTP
Page 12/13

[Now go to Section 2]

Section 2: Human Environments

Total marks: 15
Attempt ALL questions.

MARKS | STUDENT MARGIN

Question 4

Diagram Q4: Newspaper topic

After a gap of nearly 20 years, Pakistan is once again considering whether to hold a 6th population census between November 2016 and March 2017.

Source: *Daily Pakistan Global*, 15 June 2016

Look at Diagram Q4.

Explain the problems of taking a census in a developing country such as Pakistan.

5

HTP
Page 37/38

MARKS | STUDENT MARGIN

Question 5

Diagram Q5: Quote from the United Nations Convention to Combat Desertification (UNCCD)

Land degradation affects 1.5 billion people globally.

Referring to either a rainforest or semi-arid area you have studied, discuss the impact of land degradation on the people and environment. **5**

HTP Page 49/50 and Page 53

MARKS

Question 6

Table Q6: Effect of traffic congestion in UK cities

Rank	City	Delay per year, evening peak
1	Belfast	94 hours
2	Manchester	83 hours
3	Edinburgh	82 hours
4	London	77 hours
5	Brighton/Hove	68 hours
6	Nottingham	66 hours
7	Bristol	64 hours
8	Leeds/Bradford	63 hours
9	Sheffield	62 hours
10	Leicester	60 hours

Look at Table Q6.

For any named developed world city you have studied, explain the strategies used to manage traffic congestion.

5

[Now go to Section 3]

A

Section 3: Global Issues

Total marks: 20

Attempt TWO questions.

Question 7	River Basin Management
Question 8	Development and Health
Question 9	Global Climate Change
Question 10	Trade, Aid and Geopolitics
Question 11	Energy

Question 7   River Basin Management

Diagram Q7A: Hydroelectric dam

Diagram Q7B: Map of the Omo River Valley, Ethiopia

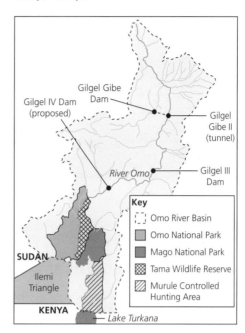

Diagram Q7C: Women collecting water from the River Omo, Ethiopia

HTP
Page 82

a) Look at Diagram Q7A.

Explain either the human or physical factors that need to be considered when selecting a site for a major dam and its associated reservoir.

5

b) Look at Diagrams Q7B and Q7C.

Referring to a water-control project that you have studied, discuss the negative environmental impacts created by the construction of a major dam and its associated reservoir.

5

A

STUDENT
MARKS   MARGIN

Question 8   Development and Health

Diagram Q8: Mobile health clinic, Mumbai, India

Look at Diagram Q8.

For a named developing country you have studied:

a) Discuss ways in which primary health care strategies can
   improve the health of the country.

b) Evaluate the effectiveness of these strategies.

HTP
Pages
99–101

6

4

	MARKS	STUDENT MARGIN

Question 9 Global Climate Change

Diagram Q9: Newspaper headline

> **Climate change threatens more than half of Scottish heritage sites**
> A new report claims that some of Scotland's most important and iconic locations could be under threat due to global warming.
> Source: *Daily Record*, 12 January 2017

Look at Diagram Q9.

a) Explain the human causes of climate change. 6

b) Discuss the possible consequences of climate change on both a local and a national scale. You should refer to examples you have studied. 4

HTP
a) Page 104
b) Page 106

Question 10   Trade, Aid and Geopolitics

Diagram Q10: The pattern of world trade

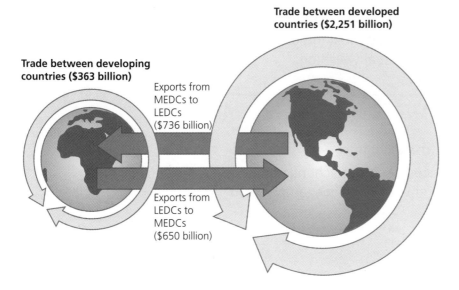

Trade between developed
countries ($2,251 billion)

Trade between developing
countries ($363 billion)

Exports from
MEDCs to
LEDCs
($736 billion)

Exports from
LEDCs to
MEDCs
($650 billion)

Study Diagram Q10.

a)   Give reasons for the inequalities in the pattern of trade shown
on the diagram.

b)   Discuss the impact that these trade patterns can have on both
developing and developed countries.

4

6

HTP
a) Page 113
b) Page 113/
114

Question 11 Energy

Diagram Q11A: UK energy production

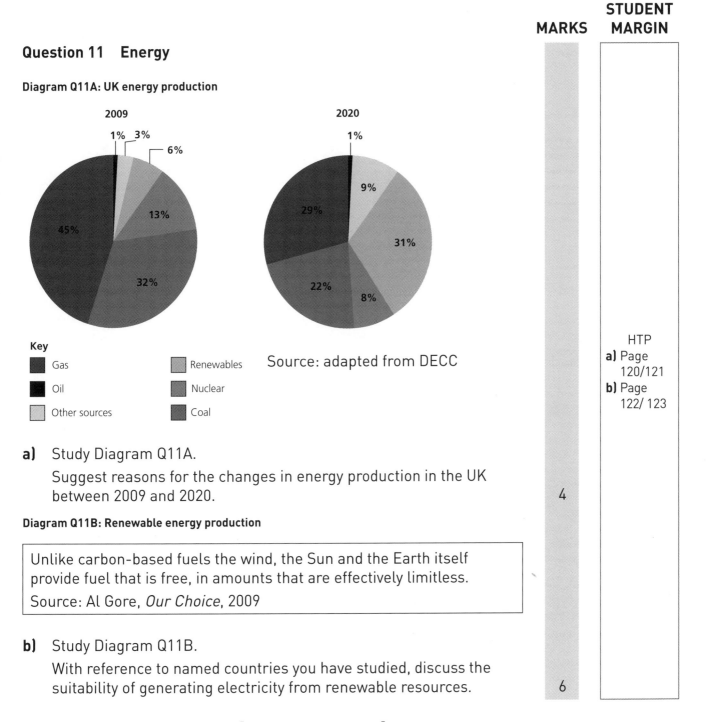

2009

1% 3%
6%
13%
45%
32%

2020

1%
9%
29%
31%
22%
8%

Key

- Gas
- Oil
- Other sources
- Renewables
- Nuclear
- Coal

Source: adapted from DECC

HTP
a) Page 120/121
b) Page 122/ 123

a) Study Diagram Q11A.

Suggest reasons for the changes in energy production in the UK between 2009 and 2020.

4

Diagram Q11B: Renewable energy production

Unlike carbon-based fuels the wind, the Sun and the Earth itself provide fuel that is free, in amounts that are effectively limitless.

Source: Al Gore, *Our Choice*, 2009

b) Study Diagram Q11B.

With reference to named countries you have studied, discuss the suitability of generating electricity from renewable resources.

6

[Now go to Section 4]

OS map showing Llanberis area

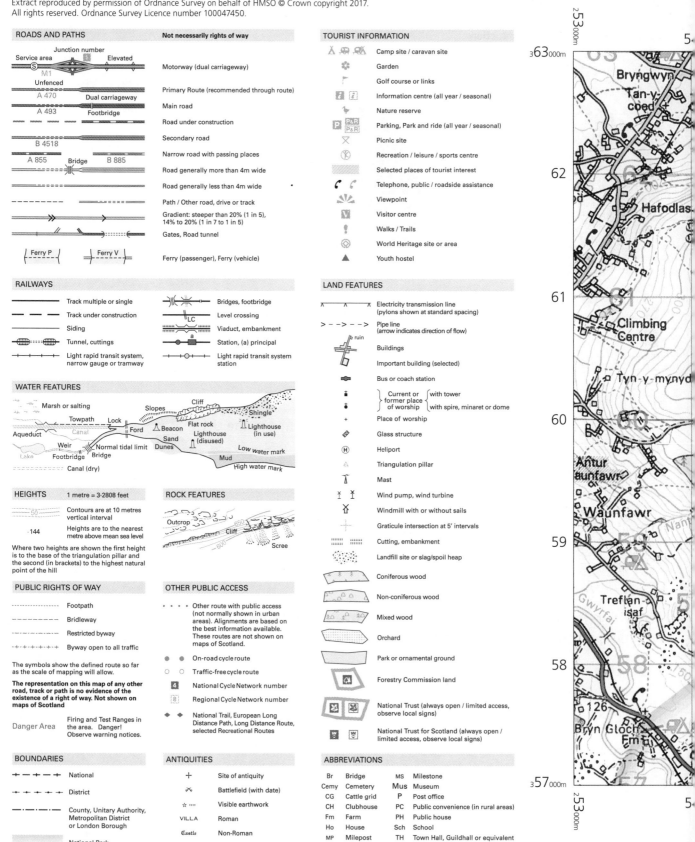

Extract reproduced by permission of Ordnance Survey on behalf of HMSO © Crown copyright 2017. All rights reserved. Ordnance Survey Licence number 100047450.

ROADS AND PATHS

Not necessarily rights of way

Junction number
Service area — Elevated
(S) M1
Unfenced
A 470 — Dual carriageway
A 493 — Footbridge

B 4518
A 855 Bridge B 885

Motorway (dual carriageway)
Primary Route (recommended through route)
Main road
Road under construction
Secondary road
Narrow road with passing places
Road generally more than 4m wide
Road generally less than 4m wide
Path / Other road, drive or track
Gradient: steeper than 20% (1 in 5), 14% to 20% (1 in 7 to 1 in 5)
Gates, Road tunnel

Ferry P   Ferry V
Ferry (passenger), Ferry (vehicle)

RAILWAYS

Track multiple or single
Track under construction
Siding
Tunnel, cuttings
Light rapid transit system, narrow gauge or tramway

Bridges, footbridge
Level crossing
Viaduct, embankment
Station, (a) principal
Light rapid transit system station

WATER FEATURES

Marsh or salting
Towpath — Lock
Aqueduct — Canal
Weir
Lake — Footbridge — Bridge
Canal (dry)

Slopes — Cliff
Shingle
Ford — Beacon — Flat rock
Sand — Lighthouse (disused)
Dunes
Mud
High water mark
Low water mark
Lighthouse (in use)
Normal tidal limit

HEIGHTS

1 metre = 3·2808 feet

50 — Contours are at 10 metres vertical interval

·144 — Heights are to the nearest metre above mean sea level

Where two heights are shown the first height is to the base of the triangulation pillar and the second (in brackets) to the highest natural point of the hill

ROCK FEATURES

Outcrop
Cliff
Scree

PUBLIC RIGHTS OF WAY

.... Footpath
— — — — Bridleway
— · — · — Restricted byway
-+-+-+-+- Byway open to all traffic

The symbols show the defined route so far as the scale of mapping will allow.

The representation on this map of any other road, track or path is no evidence of the existence of a right of way. Not shown on maps of Scotland

Danger Area — Firing and Test Ranges in the area. Danger! Observe warning notices.

OTHER PUBLIC ACCESS

· · · · Other route with public access (not normally shown in urban areas). Alignments are based on the best information available. These routes are not shown on maps of Scotland.

● ● On-road cycle route
○ ○ Traffic-free cycle route
4 National Cycle Network number
8 Regional Cycle Network number

◆ ◆ National Trail, European Long Distance Path, Long Distance Route, selected Recreational Routes

BOUNDARIES

+ — + — + National
+ — + — + District
— · — · — County, Unitary Authority, Metropolitan District or London Borough
National Park

ANTIQUITIES

+ Site of antiquity
⚔ Battlefield (with date)
☆ ···· Visible earthwork
VILLA Roman
Castle Non-Roman

TOURIST INFORMATION

Camp site / caravan site
Garden
Golf course or links
Information centre (all year / seasonal)
Nature reserve
Parking, Park and ride (all year / seasonal)
Picnic site
Recreation / leisure / sports centre
Selected places of tourist interest
Telephone, public / roadside assistance
Viewpoint
Visitor centre
Walks / Trails
World Heritage site or area
Youth hostel

LAND FEATURES

Electricity transmission line (pylons shown at standard spacing)
Pipe line (arrow indicates direction of flow)
ruin
Buildings
Important building (selected)
Bus or coach station
Current or former place of worship { with tower / with spire, minaret or dome }
Place of worship
Glass structure
Heliport
Triangulation pillar
Mast
Wind pump, wind turbine
Windmill with or without sails
Graticule intersection at 5' intervals
Cutting, embankment
Landfill site or slag/spoil heap
Coniferous wood
Non-coniferous wood
Mixed wood
Orchard
Park or ornamental ground
Forestry Commission land
National Trust (always open / limited access, observe local signs)
National Trust for Scotland (always open / limited access, observe local signs)

ABBREVIATIONS

Br	Bridge	MS	Milestone
Cemy	Cemetery	Mus	Museum
CG	Cattle grid	P	Post office
CH	Clubhouse	PC	Public convenience (in rural areas)
Fm	Farm	PH	Public house
Ho	House	Sch	School
MP	Milepost	TH	Town Hall, Guildhall or equivalent

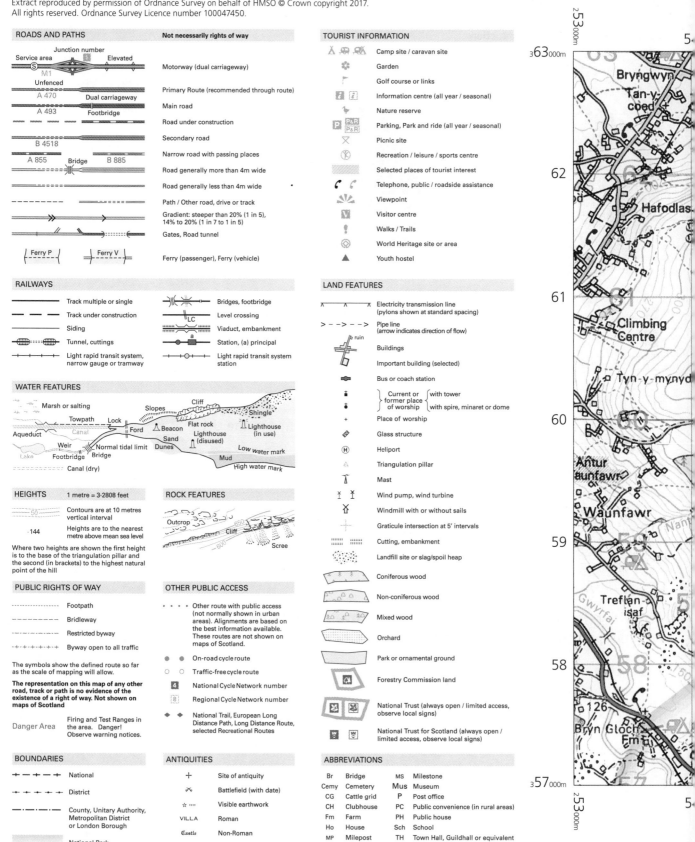

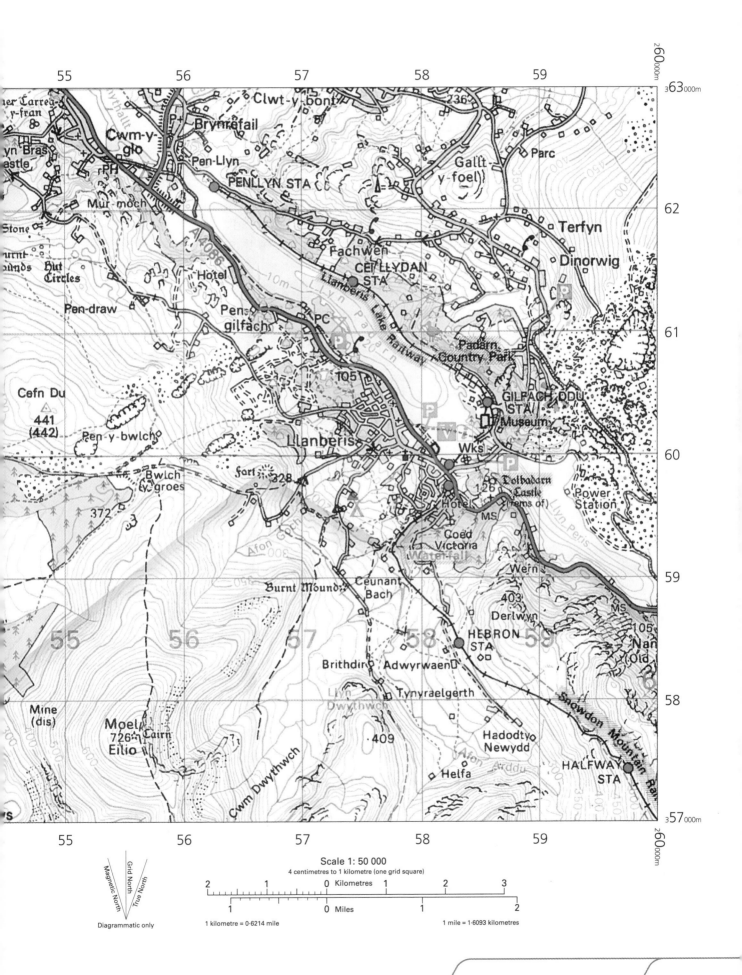

Scale 1: 50 000
4 centimetres to 1 kilometre (one grid square)

Kilometres

Miles

1 kilometre = 0·6214 mile

1 mile = 1·6093 kilometres

Grid North
Magnetic North
True North

Diagrammatic only

Section 4: Application of Geographical Skills

> **Total marks: 10**
>
> Attempt the question.

Question 12

	MARKS	STUDENT MARGIN

Controversial plans to build a £100 million hydroelectric power scheme on the edge of Snowdonia National Park have been backed by Gwynedd councillors. The proposed sites are at the old slate quarries at grid references 5460 and 5660. However, not everyone is happy with this decision.

Study the Ordnance Survey map extract of the Llanberis area, and Diagrams Q12A–Q12E, before answering this question.

Referring to evidence from the Ordnance Survey map, and other information from the sources, discuss:

a) the advantages and disadvantages of the proposed power scheme; and

b) any possible impacts on the surrounding area.

10

Diagram Q12A: Abandoned slate quarry on Cefn Du at grid reference 5460

Diagram Q12B: Climate graph for Snowdon and Llanberis

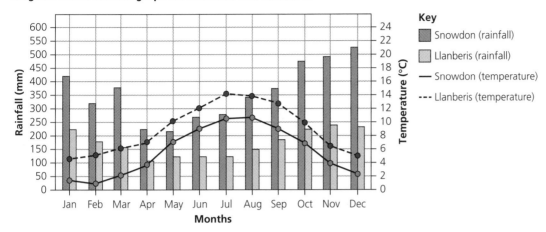

Key
- ■ Snowdon (rainfall)
- ▨ Llanberis (rainfall)
- — Snowdon (temperature)
- --- Llanberis (temperature)

Diagram Q12C: Selected facts about Snowdonia National Park

National Park	Year of designation	Population	Visitors per year	Visitor days per year	Visitor spend per year
Snowdonia	1951	25,482	4.72 million	10.4 million	£396 million

Diagram Q12D: Comment by UK Hillwalking

The impact on the environment is huge and involves ruining beautiful landscapes and wildlife breeding sites, potentially damaging lakes and water ways on both sides of the mountain, potentially unearthing unexploded munitions including nerve and mustard gas and disposing of these in the vicinity of Llanberis, three to four years of intense construction traffic causing noise and pollution and congestion of traffic in Llanberis and the surrounding area. It is poorly advertised that the view of Snowdonia currently greeting walkers and Snowdonia marathon runners ascending Cefn Du along the unnamed road to Llanberis will be replaced by a huge concrete dam stretching from the presently forested area to the quarry rim.

Source: adapted from www.ukhillwalking.com

Diagram Q12E: Comment by Quarry Battery Company, developer of the project

Pumped storage will both improve the supply of electricity and enable conventional power stations to be decommissioned, saving further costs and carbon emissions. QBC are now focusing on smaller sites and old quarries, where slate has been mined from the mountains over the past 100 years.

Source: adapted from www.quarrybatterycompany.com

[End of Practice Paper A]

Higher
Geography

Duration: 2 hours and 15 minutes

Total marks: 60

Section 1 – PHYSICAL ENVIRONMENTS – 15 MARKS

Attempt ALL questions.

Section 2 – HUMAN ENVIRONMENTS – 15 MARKS

Attempt ALL questions.

Section 3 – GLOBAL ISSUES – 20 MARKS

Attempt TWO questions.

Section 4 – APPLICATION OF GEOGRAPHICAL SKILLS – 10 MARKS

Attempt the question.

Credit will be given for appropriately labelled sketch maps and diagrams.

Write your answers clearly in the spaces provided in this paper. You must clearly identify the question number you are attempting.

Use **blue** or **black** ink.

Section 1: Physical Environments

Total marks: 15

Attempt ALL questions.

MARKS

STUDENT
MARGIN

Question 1

Diagram Q1: A selected factor affecting a hydrograph

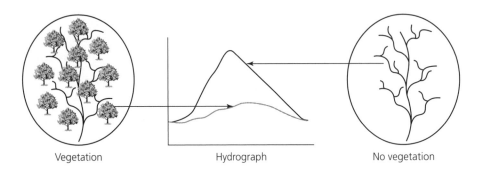

Vegetation   Hydrograph   No vegetation

Look at Diagram Q1.

Discuss the various factors, including vegetation, which can affect a
hydrograph.

5

HTP
Page 15/16

Question 2   Explain, with the aid of a diagram(s), how one of the
following features is formed:

- terminal moraine
- drumlin
- esker

HTP
Page 20/21

5

Question 3

Source: adapted from SQA Higher Geography past paper 2016

Diagram Q3A: Location of selected air masses, monthly rainfall and the ITCZ in January and July

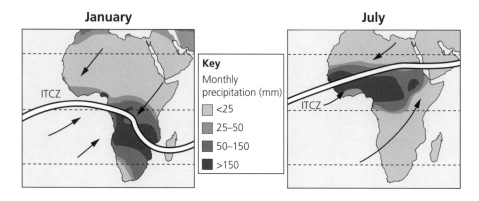

Diagram Q3B: Map of West Africa

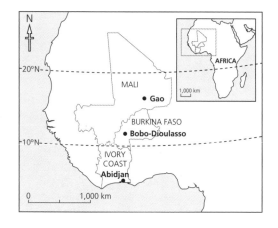

Diagram Q3C: Average monthly rainfall/days with precipitation

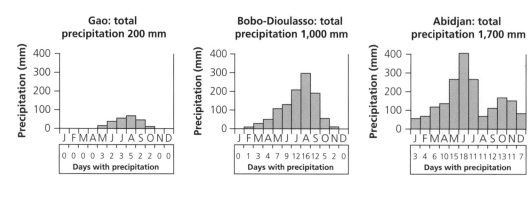

Study Diagrams Q3A, Q3B and Q3C.

Compare the rainfall patterns across West Africa and explain the variation in rainfall within West Africa.

HTP
Pages 8–10

5

[Now go to Section 2]

Section 2: Human Environments

Total marks: 15

Attempt ALL questions.

MARKS | STUDENT MARGIN

Question 4

Diagram Q4: Migrants: country of origin

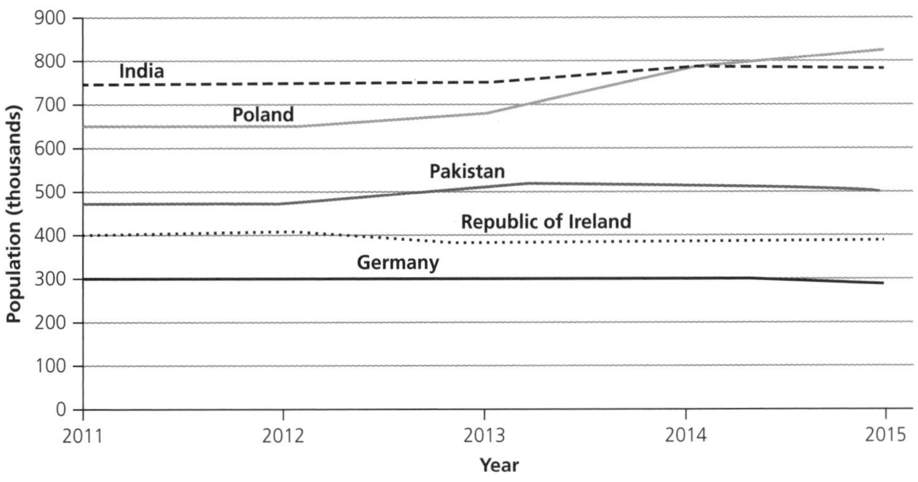

Look at Diagram Q4.

With reference to a migration flow you have studied, explain the impact on the receiving country. 5

HTP Page 45/46

Question 5

Diagram Q5: Effects of rural land degradation

Look at Diagram Q5.

Referring to either a rainforest or a semi-arid area you have studied, explain the strategies used to reduce rural land degradation.

HTP
Page 54/55

6

Question 6

Diagram Q6: A shanty town

Look at Diagram Q6.

For a named area you have studied, discuss strategies used to improve shanty towns.

[Now go to Section 3]

HTP
Page 67/68

4

B

Section 3: Global Issues

Total marks: 20

Attempt TWO questions.

Question 7	River Basin Management
Question 8	Development and Health
Question 9	Global Climate Change
Question 10	Trade, Aid and Geopolitics
Question 11	Energy

Question 7   River Basin Management

Diagram Q7A: Map of the Missouri River Basin, USA

Diagram Q7B: Selected facts for the Missouri River Basin

- Temperatures are projected to increase by roughly 2 °C during the twenty-first century.
- Precipitation is projected to remain variable with a slight increase across the basin by 2070.
- Moisture falling as rain instead of snow at lower levels is projected to increase the winter run-off, with decreased run-off during the summer.
- The population of the Missouri River Basin shows a steady increase year on year.

Diagram Q7C: Temperatures in North America during July 2016

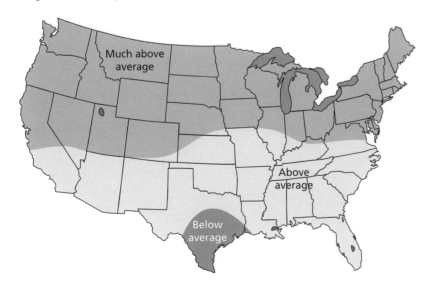

STUDENT
MARKS   MARGIN

Diagram Q7D: Annual hydrograph above Garrison Dam

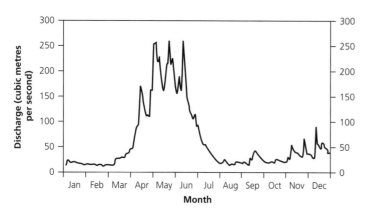

Study Diagrams Q7A, Q7B, Q7C and Q7D.

a)   Explain why there is a need for water management in the
Missouri River Basin.

b)   For any named water management scheme you have studied,
explain the positive impact on the people and environment of
the area.

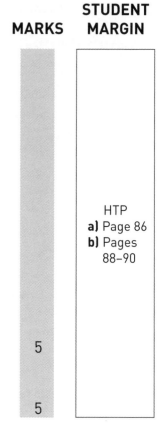

5

5

HTP
a) Page 86
b) Pages
88–90

Question 8   Development and Health

For malaria, cholera or bilharzia:

a) Explain efforts used to combat the disease.

b) Evaluate how successful these measures have been.

6

4

HTP
Pages
95–99

Question 9   Global Climate Change

Diagram Q9: Statement on global climate change

2016 world's hottest year on record, says UN

Look at Diagram Q9.

a) Discuss ways in which people can attempt to reduce global climate change.

b) Evaluate the effectiveness of these attempts.

MARKS

6

4

STUDENT MARGIN

HTP
Page 107

Question 10   Trade, Aid and Geopolitics

Diagram Q10: G7 members

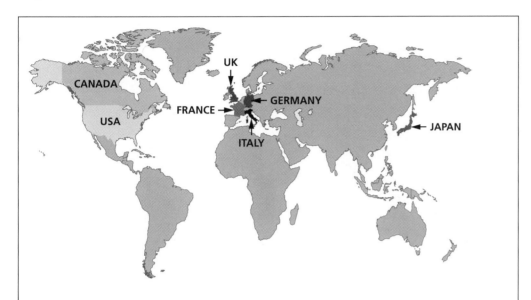

Trade is the exchange of goods and services between countries. More than half the world's trade takes place between just seven countries known as the G7. The G7 includes some of the richest and most industrialised countries in the world.

Study Diagram Q10.

a) 'Poor countries lose the most through unfair trade deals.'

Explain the impacts of unfair trade on people and countries in the developing world.

b) Discuss strategies that can be used to reduce inequalities in world trade.

HTP
a) Page 111/112
b) Page 114/115

6

4

B

Question 11 Energy

Diagram Q11A: Projection of growing world energy consumption

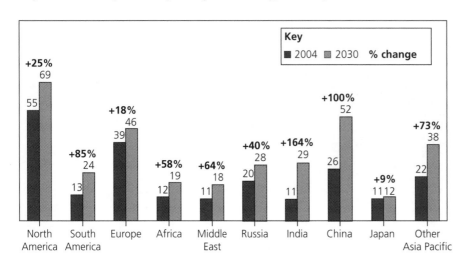

a) Look at Diagram Q11A.

Explain the reasons for the increase in energy consumption for either the developed or the developing areas of the world.

HTP
Page 121

6

Diagram Q11B: Newspaper headline

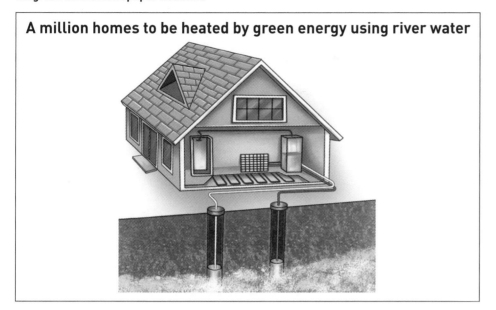

A million homes to be heated by green energy using river water

b) Look at Diagram Q11B.

Discuss the advantages of using rivers, or any other source of renewable energy you have studied, in achieving the energy demands of a country.

[Now go to Section 4]

4

HTP
Page 122

OS map showing Balmaha area
Extract reproduced by permission of Ordnance Survey on behalf of HMSO © Crown copyright 2017.
All rights reserved. Ordnance Survey Licence number 100047450.

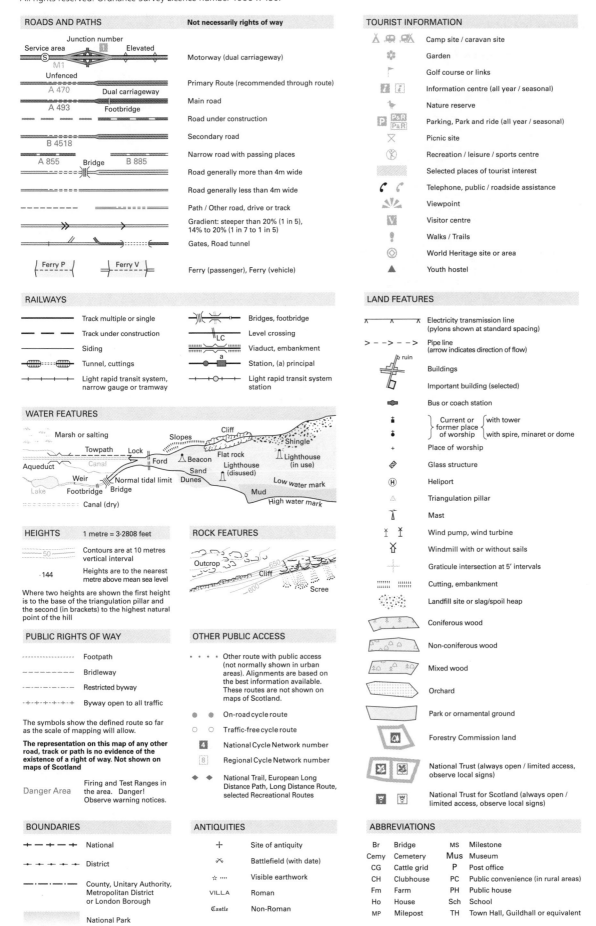

ROADS AND PATHS

Not necessarily rights of way

Junction number
Service area Elevated
Motorway (dual carriageway)

Unfenced
A 470
Primary Route (recommended through route)

Dual carriageway
A 493
Main road

Footbridge
Road under construction

Secondary road
B 4518

Narrow road with passing places

A 855 Bridge B 885
Road generally more than 4m wide

Road generally less than 4m wide

Path / Other road, drive or track

Gradient: steeper than 20% (1 in 5),
14% to 20% (1 in 7 to 1 in 5)

Gates, Road tunnel

Ferry P Ferry V
Ferry (passenger), Ferry (vehicle)

RAILWAYS

Track multiple or single
Bridges, footbridge

Track under construction
Level crossing

Siding
LC
Viaduct, embankment

Tunnel, cuttings
a
Station, (a) principal

Light rapid transit system,
narrow gauge or tramway
Light rapid transit system
station

WATER FEATURES

Marsh or salting

Cliff
Slopes
Shingle
Towpath Lock
Aqueduct Canal
Flat rock
Beacon
Ford
Lighthouse
Sand
Lighthouse (in use)
Weir
Lighthouse (disused)
Lake Footbridge Bridge Normal tidal limit
Dunes
Low water mark
Mud
High water mark

Canal (dry)

HEIGHTS

1 metre = 3·2808 feet

50
Contours are at 10 metres
vertical interval

·144
Heights are to the nearest
metre above mean sea level

Where two heights are shown the first height
is to the base of the triangulation pillar and
the second (in brackets) to the highest natural
point of the hill

ROCK FEATURES

Outcrop
650
Cliff
600
Scree

PUBLIC RIGHTS OF WAY

············ Footpath

─ ─ ─ ─ ─ Bridleway

─·─·─·─·─ Restricted byway

─+─+─+─+─ Byway open to all traffic

The symbols show the defined route so far
as the scale of mapping will allow.

**The representation on this map of any other
road, track or path is no evidence of the
existence of a right of way. Not shown on
maps of Scotland**

Danger Area
Firing and Test Ranges in
the area. Danger!
Observe warning notices.

OTHER PUBLIC ACCESS

• • • • Other route with public access
(not normally shown in urban
areas). Alignments are based on
the best information available.
These routes are not shown on
maps of Scotland.

● ● On-road cycle route

○ ○ Traffic-free cycle route

4 National Cycle Network number

8 Regional Cycle Network number

◆ ◆ National Trail, European Long
Distance Path, Long Distance Route,
selected Recreational Routes

TOURIST INFORMATION

Camp site / caravan site

Garden

Golf course or links

Information centre (all year / seasonal)

Nature reserve

Parking, Park and ride (all year / seasonal)

Picnic site

Recreation / leisure / sports centre

Selected places of tourist interest

Telephone, public / roadside assistance

Viewpoint

Visitor centre

Walks / Trails

World Heritage site or area

Youth hostel

LAND FEATURES

Electricity transmission line
(pylons shown at standard spacing)

Pipe line
(arrow indicates direction of flow)

ruin
Buildings

Important building (selected)

Bus or coach station

Current or
former place
of worship
with tower
with spire, minaret or dome

+ Place of worship

Glass structure

(H) Heliport

△ Triangulation pillar

Mast

Wind pump, wind turbine

Windmill with or without sails

Graticule intersection at 5' intervals

Cutting, embankment

Landfill site or slag/spoil heap

Coniferous wood

Non-coniferous wood

Mixed wood

Orchard

Park or ornamental ground

Forestry Commission land

National Trust (always open / limited access,
observe local signs)

National Trust for Scotland (always open /
limited access, observe local signs)

BOUNDARIES

─+─ ─ ─+─ National

─+·+·+·+─ District

─────── County, Unitary Authority,
Metropolitan District
or London Borough

National Park

ANTIQUITIES

+ Site of antiquity

⚔ Battlefield (with date)

☆ ···· Visible earthwork

VILLA Roman

Castle Non-Roman

ABBREVIATIONS

Br	Bridge	MS	Milestone
Cemy	Cemetery	Mus	Museum
CG	Cattle grid	P	Post office
CH	Clubhouse	PC	Public convenience (in rural areas)
Fm	Farm	PH	Public house
Ho	House	Sch	School
MP	Milepost	TH	Town Hall, Guildhall or equivalent

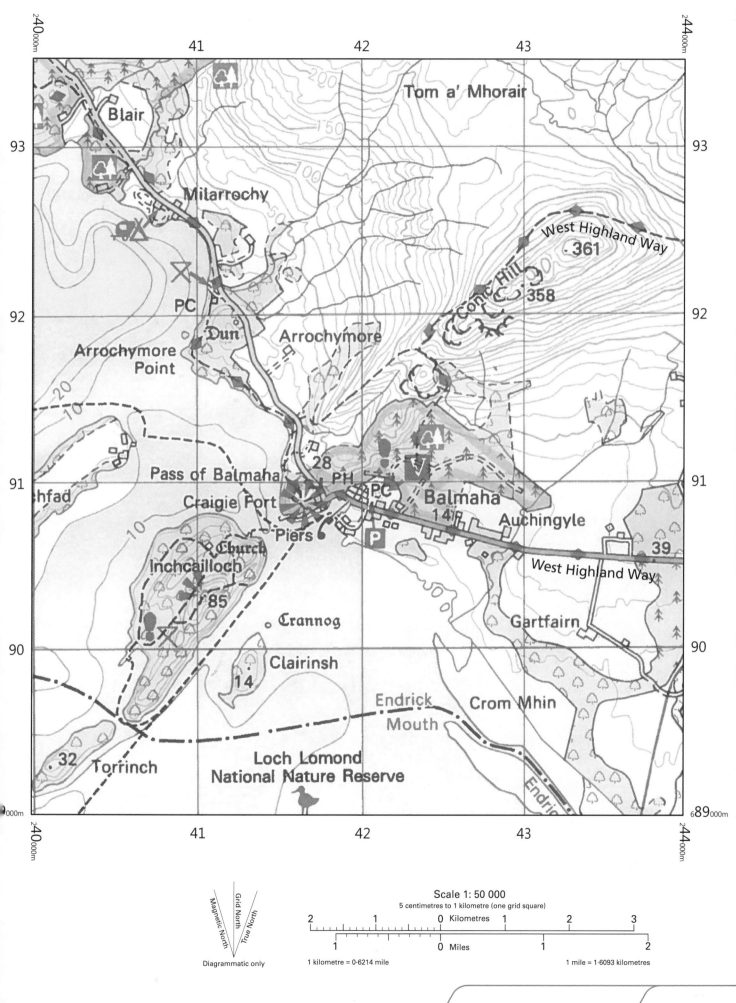

Scale 1: 50 000
5 centimetres to 1 kilometre (one grid square)

Magnetic North Grid North True North

Diagrammatic only

2   1   0   Kilometres   1   2   3

1   0   Miles   1   2

1 kilometre = 0·6214 mile   1 mile = 1·6093 kilometres

Section 4: Application of Geographical Skills

Total marks: 10

Attempt the question.

MARKS	STUDENT MARGIN

Question 12

A plan to build 22 new houses at Balmaha within the Loch Lomond and The Trossachs National Park has been proposed.

Study the Ordnance Survey map extract of the Balmaha area, Diagram Q12, and Diagrams Q12A–D before answering this question.

Referring to evidence from the Ordnance Survey map, and other information from the sources, discuss:

a) the advantages and disadvantages of the proposed housing development; and

b) any possible impacts on the surrounding area.

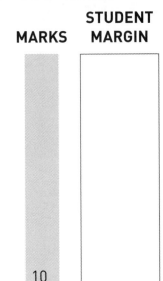

10

Diagram Q12: Proposed site of new housing in Balmaha

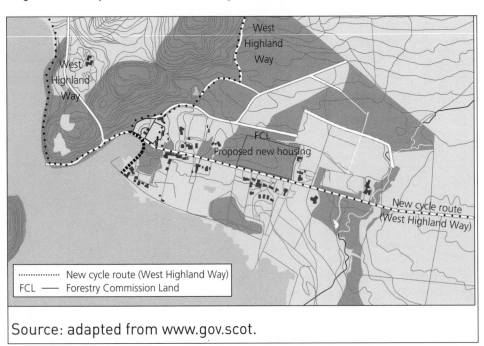

Source: adapted from www.gov.scot.

Diagram Q12A: Proposed housing development at Balmaha

It is proposed to build 22 houses on a 5-acre woodland site owned by the Forestry Commission, close to the West Highland Way. Twenty of the houses will be a modest size and will be affordable homes for young people, families and older people. Two of the plots will be for private sale. The housing will be eco-friendly and blend in with its surroundings, and screened from the road by trees.

Diagram Q12B: The West Highland Way

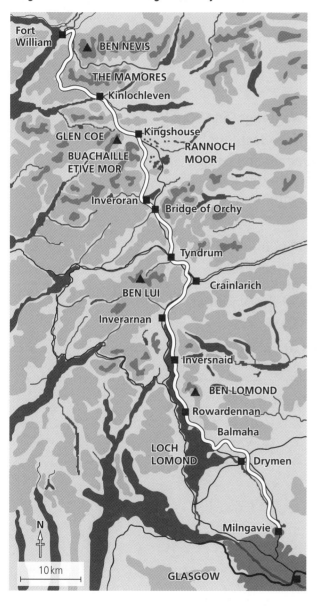

The West Highland Way is one of Scotland's premier walking routes and welcomes around 85,000 visitors every year. Extending from Milngavie up to Fort William, at the foot of Ben Nevis, this 96-mile route provides breathtaking scenery and spectacular wildlife along the way.

The West Highland Way generates some £3.5 million for the Scottish economy each year. For some businesses along its route, such as the Oak Tree Inn at Balmaha, 100 per cent of their income is generated from this source.

Diagram Q12C: Views of the Balmaha Biodiversity Community Action (BBCA) group

A local community group, Balmaha Biodiversity Community Action (BBCA), has been formed to protect the wild woodland site that has been proposed for development.

The BCCA chairman stated that: 'The ancient woodland in Balmaha is extremely valuable ... Several rare and protected species can be found on the land; otters nest there as do red squirrel, we have a healthy colony of endangered slow-worms – all of which are protected. Building these houses will ruin this precious habitat and what is recognised by the Loch Lomond and The Trossachs National Park as one of the main tourist draws to the area [the West Highland Way].'

Diagram Q12D: Newspaper headline

Proposed Balmaha housing would be no threat to the West Highland Way

Balmaha, like many other small rural communities in the National Park, is facing major challenges in retaining young people and people of working age, due to the lack of affordable housing with tourism operators and well-heeled commuters and retirees continuing to snap up any housing that comes on the market.

It is important the National Park is a place for people of all ages and socio-economic backgrounds, as well as nature and this modest social housing development will help achieve this. The development of new affordable housing is part of the future plans of the National Park authority.

Source: letter from James Fraser, Chairman Friends of Loch Lomond and The Trossachs to *The Herald*, 27 January 2017

[End of Practice Paper B]

Higher
Geography

C

Duration: 2 hours and 15 minutes

Total marks: 60

Section 1 – PHYSICAL ENVIRONMENTS – 15 MARKS

Attempt ALL questions.

Section 2 – HUMAN ENVIRONMENTS – 15 MARKS

Attempt ALL questions.

Section 3 – GLOBAL ISSUES – 20 MARKS

Attempt TWO questions.

Section 4 – APPLICATION OF GEOGRAPHICAL SKILLS – 10 MARKS

Attempt the question.

Credit will be given for appropriately labelled sketch maps and diagrams.

Write your answers clearly in the spaces provided in this paper. You must clearly identify the question number you are attempting.

Use **blue** or **black** ink.

Section 1: Physical Environments

Total marks: 15

Attempt ALL questions.

MARKS

STUDENT MARGIN

Question 1

Diagram Q1: A soil profile

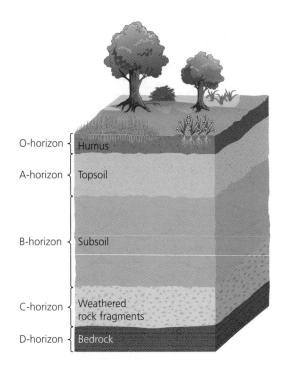

O-horizon { Humus

A-horizon { Topsoil

B-horizon { Subsoil

C-horizon { Weathered rock fragments

D-horizon { Bedrock

Look at Diagram Q1.

With the aid of a diagram, explain the formation of a podzol. You should refer to the characteristics of the soil including horizons, colour, soil biota, texture and drainage.

5

HTP Page 34

Question 2

Diagram Q2: Corrie formation

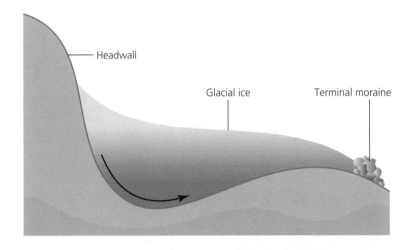

Look at Diagram Q2.

Explain, in detail, the processes involved in the formation of a corrie.
You may wish to use a diagram(s) in your answer.

MARKS

STUDENT
MARGIN

HTP
Page 20

5

Question 3

Diagram Q3: Possible land uses in Loch Lomond and The Trossachs National Park

Recreation and tourism

Forestry and renewable energy

Farming and industry

Water storage and supply

Look at Diagram Q3.

Referring to a glaciated upland area you have studied, explain the environmental conflicts caused by the various land uses.

[Now go to Section 2]

5

HTP
Pages
24–27

Section 2: Human Environments

> **Total marks: 15**
>
> Attempt ALL questions.

Question 4

Diagram Q4: Population structure of India in 2010 and 2050 (projected)

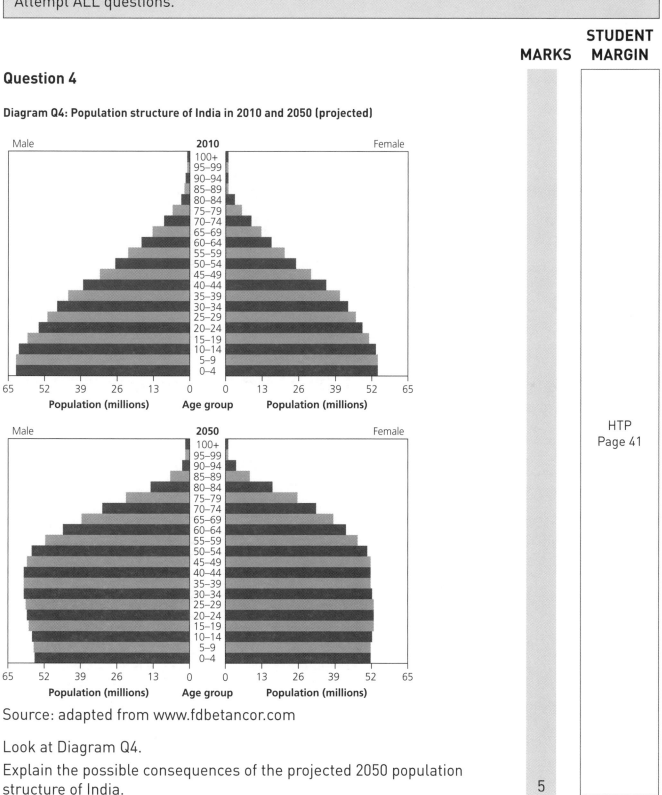

Source: adapted from www.fdbetancor.com

Look at Diagram Q4.

Explain the possible consequences of the projected 2050 population structure of India.

5

C

Question 5

For a named rainforest or semi-arid area you have studied, evaluate strategies used to reduce the impact of land degradation on the people and the environment.

STUDENT
MARKS   MARGIN

Question 6

Diagram Q6: Demolition of Red Road Flats, Glasgow

Look at Diagram Q6.

For a named developed world city you have studied, explain the need for housing management.

You should refer to specific named examples from your chosen city.

HTP
Page 60/61

5

[Now go to Section 3]

C

Section 3: Global Issues

Total marks: 20

Attempt TWO questions.

Question 7	River Basin Management
Question 8	Development and Health
Question 9	Global Climate Change
Question 10	Trade, Aid and Geopolitics
Question 11	Energy

Question 7   River Basin Management

Diagram Q7A: Possible sites for a dam

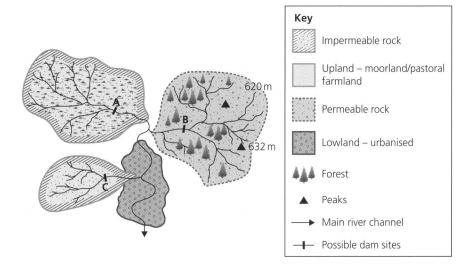

Key

▨	Impermeable rock
▢	Upland – moorland/pastoral farmland
▨	Permeable rock
▨	Lowland – urbanised
🌲🌲🌲	Forest
▲	Peaks
→	Main river channel
—∣—	Possible dam sites

620 m
▲632 m

Source: adapted from SQA Intermediate 2 paper 2013

a) Look at Diagram Q7A.

Evaluate the suitability of sites A, B and C for the location of a dam.

5

HTP
a) Page 80/81
b) Pages 82/87–88/90

Diagram Q7B: Rainbow Bridge on the Colorado River, USA

b) Look at Diagram Q7B.

For any river basin scheme you have studied, discuss the environmental impacts of damming a river.

5

Question 8   Development and Health

a) Discuss the validity of using composite indicators, such as the Physical Quality of Life Index (PQLI).

4

Diagram Q8: Selected indicators of development for India and Afghanistan

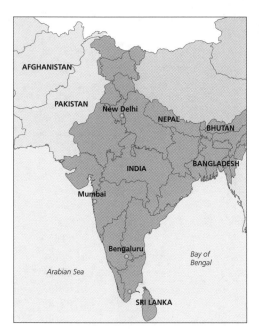

Indicator	India	Afghanistan
GNI per capita	$6,030	$1,940
Life expectancy	68	60.5
Under-five mortality rate (per 1,000)	47	91.1
Access to water	91.1%	55.3%

HTP
a) Page 93
b) Page 94

b) Study Diagram Q8.

Suggest reasons for the differences in levels of development that exist between developing countries. You may wish to refer to countries you have studied.

6

Question 9   Global Climate Change

Diagram Q9: Global climate change

HTP
a) Page 104
b) Page
105/106

Look at Diagram Q9.

a) Explain the physical factors that have contributed to global climate change.

b) Discuss the global effects of climate change.

4

6

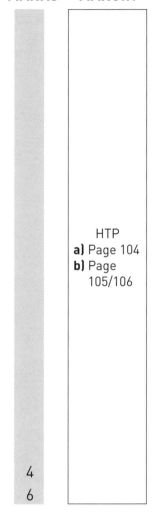

C

Question 10   Trade, Aid and Geopolitics

Diagram Q10: Commodity prices 2012–16

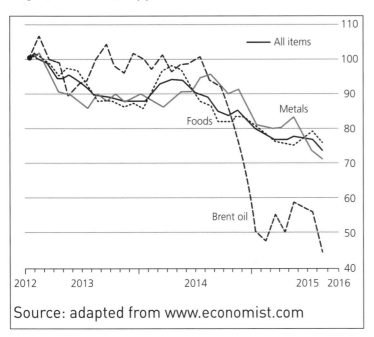

Source: adapted from www.economist.com

HTP
a) Page 112
b) Page 115

Look at Diagram Q10.

a) Evaluate the impact of changing commodity prices on people and countries in the developing world.

4

b) Explain how fair trade can improve the lives of people in developing countries.

6

Question 11 Energy

Diagram Q11A: Non-renewable energy sources

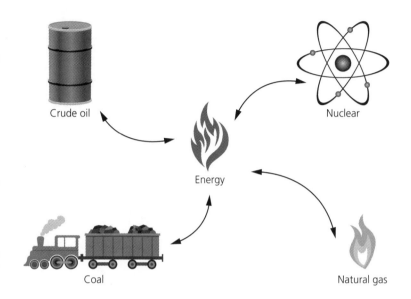

Crude oil

Nuclear

Energy

Coal

Natural gas

a) Look at Diagram Q11A.

Evaluate the effectiveness of using non-renewable energy sources to meet energy demands.

Diagram Q11B: Growth in energy demand

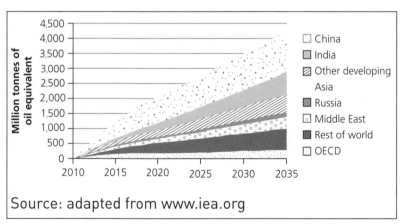

Source: adapted from www.iea.org

b) Study Diagram Q11B.

Discuss the growth in demand for energy between 2010 and 2035.

[Now go to Section 4]

HTP
a) Page 121/122
b) Page 120/121

5

5

OS map showing Stornoway area
Extract reproduced by permission of Ordnance Survey on behalf of HMSO © Crown copyright 2017.
All rights reserved. Ordnance Survey Licence number 100047450.

ROADS AND PATHS

Not necessarily rights of way

Service area — Junction number — Elevated — S — M1	Motorway (dual carriageway)
Unfenced — A 470 — Dual carriageway	Primary Route (recommended through route)
A 493 — Footbridge	Main road
	Road under construction
B 4518	Secondary road
A 855 — Bridge — B 885	Narrow road with passing places
	Road generally more than 4m wide
	Road generally less than 4m wide
	Path / Other road, drive or track
	Gradient: steeper than 20% (1 in 5), 14% to 20% (1 in 7 to 1 in 5)
	Gates, Road tunnel
Ferry P — Ferry V	Ferry (passenger), Ferry (vehicle)

RAILWAYS

Track multiple or single		Bridges, footbridge	
Track under construction		Level crossing	LC
Siding		Viaduct, embankment	
Tunnel, cuttings		Station, (a) principal	a
Light rapid transit system, narrow gauge or tramway		Light rapid transit system station	

WATER FEATURES

Marsh or salting · Slopes · Cliff · Towpath · Lock · Shingle · Aqueduct · Canal · Ford · Beacon · Flat rock · Lighthouse · Lighthouse (in use) · Weir · Sand · Lighthouse (disused) · Low water mark · Lake · Footbridge · Normal tidal limit · Bridge · Dunes · Mud · High water mark · Canal (dry)

HEIGHTS

1 metre = 3·2808 feet

Contours are at 10 metres vertical interval

·144 Heights are to the nearest metre above mean sea level

Where two heights are shown the first height is to the base of the triangulation pillar and the second (in brackets) to the highest natural point of the hill

ROCK FEATURES

Outcrop · Cliff · Scree

PUBLIC RIGHTS OF WAY

· · · · · · · ·	Footpath
– – – – – –	Bridleway
– · – · – · –	Restricted byway
–+–+–+–+	Byway open to all traffic

The symbols show the defined route so far as the scale of mapping will allow.

The representation on this map of any other road, track or path is no evidence of the existence of a right of way. Not shown on maps of Scotland

Danger Area — Firing and Test Ranges in the area. Danger! Observe warning notices.

OTHER PUBLIC ACCESS

• • • •	Other route with public access (not normally shown in urban areas). Alignments are based on the best information available. These routes are not shown on maps of Scotland.
●	On-road cycle route
○	Traffic-free cycle route
4	National Cycle Network number
8	Regional Cycle Network number
◆ ◆	National Trail, European Long Distance Path, Long Distance Route, selected Recreational Routes

BOUNDARIES

–+–+–+–	National
–+–+–+–	District
–·–·–·–	County, Unitary Authority, Metropolitan District or London Borough
	National Park

ANTIQUITIES

✛	Site of antiquity
⚔	Battlefield (with date)
☆ ⚬⚬⚬	Visible earthwork
VILLA	Roman
Castle	Non-Roman

TOURIST INFORMATION

Ⓧ ⛺ 🚐	Camp site / caravan site
✿	Garden
⛳	Golf course or links
🏛 ℹ	Information centre (all year / seasonal)
🦌	Nature reserve
P P&R	Parking, Park and ride (all year / seasonal)
⚔	Picnic site
⊗	Recreation / leisure / sports centre
▨▨▨	Selected places of tourist interest
☎ ☎	Telephone, public / roadside assistance
☼	Viewpoint
V	Visitor centre
!	Walks / Trails
⊚	World Heritage site or area
▲	Youth hostel

LAND FEATURES

┬───┬───┬	Electricity transmission line (pylons shown at standard spacing)
> – – > – – >	Pipe line (arrow indicates direction of flow)
⊣ ruin	Buildings
▪	Important building (selected)
⬭	Bus or coach station
▮ } Current or former place with tower	
▮ } of worship with spire, minaret or dome	
+	Place of worship
⬨	Glass structure
Ⓗ	Heliport
△	Triangulation pillar
⊤	Mast
⚹ ⊤	Wind pump, wind turbine
⚒	Windmill with or without sails
+	Graticule intersection at 5' intervals
▥▥▥	Cutting, embankment
⣿	Landfill site or slag/spoil heap
✿✿	Coniferous wood
⚘⚘	Non-coniferous wood
⚘✿	Mixed wood
◌◌	Orchard
	Park or ornamental ground
Ⓐ	Forestry Commission land
▦ ▦	National Trust (always open / limited access, observe local signs)
▦ ▦	National Trust for Scotland (always open / limited access, observe local signs)

ABBREVIATIONS

Br	Bridge	MS	Milestone
Cemy	Cemetery	Mus	Museum
CG	Cattle grid	P	Post office
CH	Clubhouse	PC	Public convenience (in rural areas)
Fm	Farm	PH	Public house
Ho	House	Sch	School
MP	Milepost	TH	Town Hall, Guildhall or equivalent

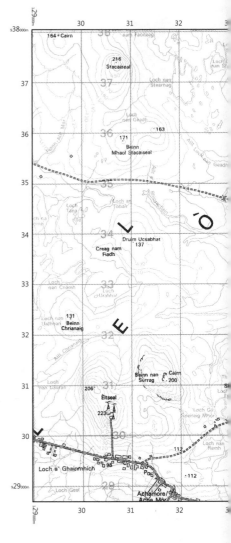

Magnetic North · Grid North · True North

Diagrammatic only

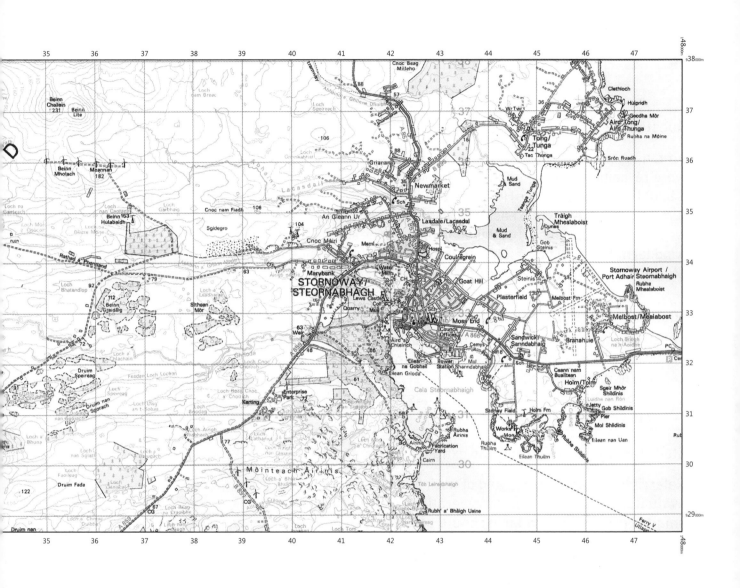

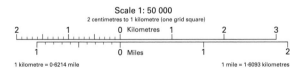

Scale 1: 50 000

2 centimetres to 1 kilometre (one grid square)

Kilometres

Miles

1 kilometre = 0·6214 mile   1 mile = 1·6093 kilometres

Section 4: Application of Geographical Skills

Total marks: 10

Attempt the question.

MARKS

STUDENT
MARGIN

Question 12

Ambitious plans to build the largest wind farm in the whole of Europe were revealed in 2004. The wind farm was proposed to be sited on the Isle of Lewis in the Outer Hebrides of Scotland. It was suggested that 234 turbines be constructed, each at 135 metres high. Planning permission was denied for such a large wind farm, however a smaller 42-turbine wind farm has now been suggested to be sited just outside the town of Stornoway. This would be known as the Stornoway Wind Farm.

Considerations when siting a wind farm:

- adequate wind – at least 11 miles per hour on average
- impact on environment, plant and animal life
- visual and noise pollution
- impact on Scotland's greenhouse gas emissions
- impact on the local economy

Study the Ordnance Survey map extract and Diagrams Q12A–Q12F.

Referring to map evidence and other information from the sources, **evaluate**, in relation to the considerations above, **whether the smaller proposed wind farm should be given planning permission**.

10

Diagram Q12A: Average wind speed for the Isle of Lewis (2015)

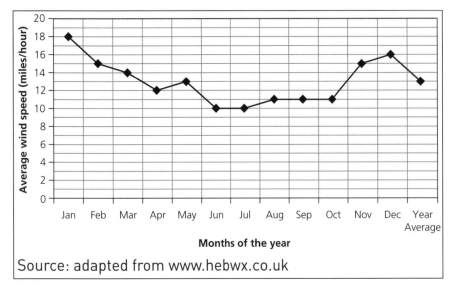

Source: adapted from www.hebwx.co.uk

Diagram Q12B: Extract from www.rspb.org.uk, The Royal Society for the Protection of Birds

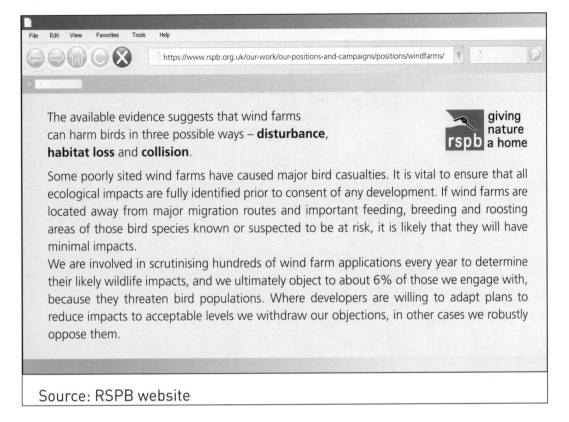

Source: RSPB website

Diagram Q12C: Proposed site of wind farm, detail from OS map of Stornoway area
Map extract reproduced by permission © Crown copyright 2017 Ordnance Survey Licence no. 100047450.

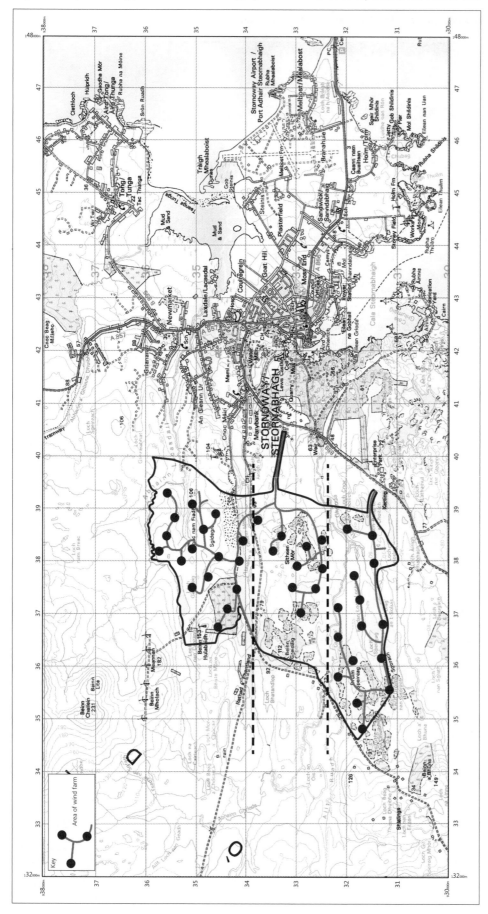

Diagram Q12D: Views of locals

Charlie Macleod – Village resident

The turbines are placed very close to the settlements because the centre of the proposed wind farm area is peatland moor and a Special Area of Conservation. The turbines are huge and will dominate the landscape. Video evidence shows them to be extremely noisy.

Angus Campbell – Councillor

There are few opportunities for employment in the area so the wind farm will bring jobs and money to the region. The community will receive benefits estimated at £566,000. Stornoway Wind is offering between £2m and £3.5m in annual rental income to the crofters whose animals graze on the land supporting the wind farm.

Eilidh McKinnon – Crofter

My family have lived and worked on the land here for over one hundred years. We are part of the land. The wind farm will destroy the moor and threaten our traditional way of life. The money offered to the community is nothing more than a bribe.

Diagram Q12E: A leaflet given to residents of Lewis by Stornoway Wind, the company responsible for the proposed wind farm

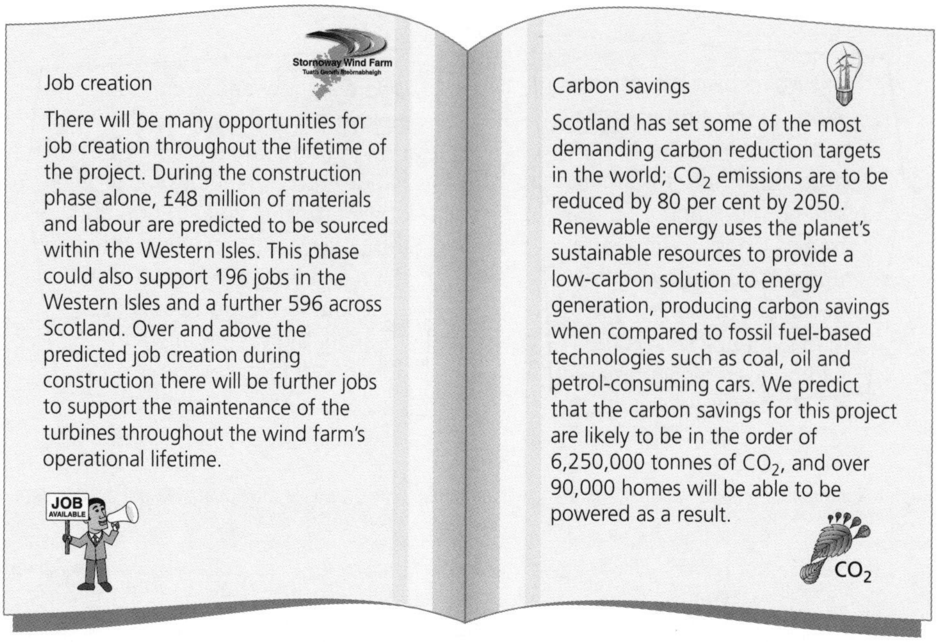

Stornoway Wind Farm

Job creation

There will be many opportunities for job creation throughout the lifetime of the project. During the construction phase alone, £48 million of materials and labour are predicted to be sourced within the Western Isles. This phase could also support 196 jobs in the Western Isles and a further 596 across Scotland. Over and above the predicted job creation during construction there will be further jobs to support the maintenance of the turbines throughout the wind farm's operational lifetime.

JOB AVAILABLE

Carbon savings

Scotland has set some of the most demanding carbon reduction targets in the world; CO_2 emissions are to be reduced by 80 per cent by 2050. Renewable energy uses the planet's sustainable resources to provide a low-carbon solution to energy generation, producing carbon savings when compared to fossil fuel-based technologies such as coal, oil and petrol-consuming cars. We predict that the carbon savings for this project are likely to be in the order of 6,250,000 tonnes of CO_2, and over 90,000 homes will be able to be powered as a result.

CO_2

Source: www.stornoway.com © Stornoway Wind Farm

[End of Practice Paper C]

Higher
Geography

Practice Paper A

Section 1: Physical Environments

1   **Hint:** Avoid a simple list of points. You need to give reasons for the differences. Well-annotated diagrams with reasons can gain full marks.

Places nearer or further from the Equator have different temperatures because of the angle at which the Sun's rays strike the surface of the Earth **(1)**. Between the Equator and the tropics the Sun's rays have less atmosphere to travel through, so less energy is lost through absorption and reflection by clouds, dust and gas **(1)**. The rays of the Sun cover a smaller area here so are more concentrated, making the intensity of insolation higher **(1)**. At the poles the Earth is tilting away from the Sun; the Sun's rays have to travel further through the atmosphere, covering a larger area, so insolation is lower here **(1)**. At the tropics areas of dense vegetation, such as the rainforest, absorb radiation; the poles are covered in snow and ice, which reflect the incoming radiation back into the atmosphere **(1)**.   **5 marks**

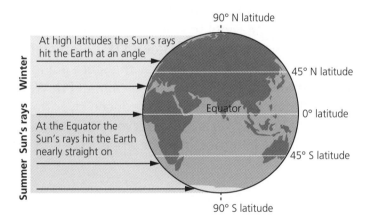

2   **Hint:** If the question specifically asks for a diagram then you could lose a mark for not using one. Well-annotated diagrams can gain full marks. Explaining processes in detail can gain marks. Avoid descriptive answers as these will gain you limited marks.

Sand spits are ridges of sand or shingle that slowly extend from the shore across a bay or river estuary. They are caused by longshore drift, a process of transportation that shifts eroded material along a coastline **(1)**. This sideways movement occurs when waves, driven by the prevailing wind, push material up the beach, known as the swash **(1)**. The returning backwash is dragged back down the beach at right angles by gravity **(1)**. Material slowly builds up to appear above the water and begins to grow longer and wider. Spits develop as long as the supply of deposits is greater than the amount of erosion **(1)**. Spits form when there is a change in direction on a coastline, which allows a sheltered area for deposition and mud flats or salt marshes to form **(1)**. They can also develop at a bay or river estuary where the river current prevents the spit from extending right across the bay or estuary **(1)**. The shape can change through time to become curved or hooked at the end in response to changes in wind direction and currents **(1)**.　　　　**5 marks**

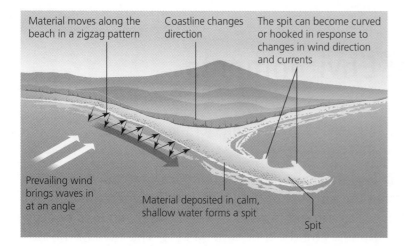

3　**Hint:** Read the question carefully. This question can be asked for human environment reasons, physical environment reasons, or both physical *and* human environment reasons.

In urban areas people remove trees and vegetation then cover soil in impermeable materials such as tarmac or concrete, which increase surface run-off **(1)**. This leads to higher river levels and increases the risk of flooding **(1)**. It also reduces the amount of water that returns to groundwater storage, possibly reducing the water table **(1)**. Deforestation means that there are no tree leaves and roots to soak up precipitation, leading to increased run-off and flooding through increased river flows **(1)**. Deforestation can lead to a decrease in evapo-transpiration rates, which means less moisture going into the atmosphere, leading to less cloud formation and therefore less rainfall **(1)**. Water removed from rivers and underground stores for irrigation results in reduced river flow and lowers the water table **(1)**. The silting-up of lakes, rivers and reservoirs due to waste products and mining processes can result in reduced storage in these areas **(1)**.　　**5 marks**

Section 2: Human Environments

4 **Hint:** The question refers to a country such as Pakistan. This is just an example, and you do not need to answer on Pakistan: use the example you have studied. The question asks for an explanation, so you need to give reasons to support your answer. If you simply describe, you may get no marks. Try to refer to specific examples in your answer. Read the question carefully as this question could be asked for either a developed or a developing country, and you would be penalised for discussing the wrong choice.

A census is expensive, involving costs of printing, distributing and analysing results that poor countries may not be able to afford **(1)**, especially with increasing populations needing housing, health care and education **(1)**. The variety of languages spoken in many countries (for example, over 500 in Nigeria) may make it difficult to provide forms that everyone can understand **(1)**. Rural–urban migration results in the creation of shanty towns, for example Makoko in Lagos, Nigeria, where many people have no address for the enumerator to deliver the census form **(1)**; people may also be homeless and sleep on the streets, or moving frequently **(1)**. In the Amazon basin the local tribes are shifting cultivators, which may result in people either being missed or counted twice **(1)**. The dense rainforest has poor access and few communication links, making it difficult for an enumerator to reach **(1)**. In countries that restrict the number of children a family can have, such as China, people may lie on the census as they are afraid they will lose benefits or have to pay extra taxes **(1)**. In Nigeria some politicians and government officials from certain regions alter the figures so that their region gets extra funds from the government, resulting in the census figures being higher than the actual population **(1)**.   **5 marks**

5 **Hint:** Avoid a simple description of the effects of land degradation. Marks will be awarded for how it impacts the people and the environment. Remember you can give both positive and negative points. For full marks you must refer to both the people and the environment. You should also refer to examples you have studied.

If rainforest chosen:

Removal of the forest for mining, logging and so on, destroys the way of life of the indigenous people. Their hunting areas may be destroyed, leaving them short of food and forcing them to move further inland **(1)**. The tribes use the land in a sustainable manner but loggers and miners destroy the area, completely preventing it from regenerating **(1)**. The using-up of tribal land resulted in the creation of reserves for the indigenous people, causing unrest and conflict with the developers **(1)**. The new settlers brought disease that the local people had no immunity to, causing large numbers to die **(1)**. Local farmers have been displaced and forced to move to crowded cities, where they end up living in favelas **(1)**.

If semi-arid area chosen:

Over-cropping and the cultivation of only one crop (monoculture) leads to nutrients being removed from the soil and results in crop failure. There has been a 25 per cent reduction in agricultural production in the Sahel since 2010 **(1)**. This has led to people being undernourished, with many dying from starvation. This has led to famine in Mauritania and Chad **(1)**. When people are undernourished, they are susceptible to diseases such as kwashiorkor; if they are sick they cannot work, so have no money to buy food **(1)**. When the crops fail, people in rural areas are forced to leave the countryside and move to the cities in search of food and employment, which results in the growth of shanty towns **(1)**.

The traditional way of life of the nomads is threatened as they cannot find food and water for their animals. Many are forced to settle in villages or at oases. This in turn puts pressure on the surrounding land, leading to over-cultivation (1). Many people become refugees as they are forced to leave their homes and seek food and shelter in neighbouring countries. This can lead to conflict with the resident populations (1). **5 marks**

6   **Hint:** Avoid giving general answers – refer to examples from a named developed city you have studied. Remember: do not just describe but give reasons for the strategies you mention in your answer.

If Glasgow chosen:

Some streets in Glasgow city centre have been pedestrianised to create traffic-free areas, for example Buchanan Street, so that the streets are no longer congested and are safer for pedestrians (1). Park and ride schemes, for example at Merriton and Chatelherault, have been introduced; people park their cars on the outskirts and travel into the city by train or bus, which now run more frequently to encourage the use of public transport, thus reducing the number of vehicles on the road (1). One-way systems, such as George Square, improve the flow of traffic and reduce congestion (1). Parking restrictions and making parking more expensive also discourage motorists from using their car in the city centre; removing on-street parking makes the streets wider, allowing traffic to flow better (1). Multi-storey car parks hold large numbers of cars, reducing congestion on the streets (1). Dedicated bus lanes reduce travelling time, making public transport more efficient (1). Improvements in the road system, with new links created to bypass congested areas, removes unnecessary traffic from narrow roads (1). **5 marks**

Section 3: Global Issues

7 **River Basin Management**

a) **Hint:** Read the question carefully. This can be asked for either human factors, physical factors, or both. If asked for both you will lose marks if you only discuss one factor. Remember to give reasons why each factor you write about is important, not just a description. Both options are shown in the sample answers below.

Physical factors might include:

The rock type must be strong and hard to withstand the weight of the water in the reservoir behind the dam **(1)**. The rock should also be impermeable so that no water is lost through seepage **(1)**. There must be a large catchment area (large river basin) to maintain a high water level in the reservoir; many streams should flow into the reservoir to provide this **(1)**. The valley should be narrow to reduce the cost of construction of the dam as river basin management schemes are expensive **(1)**. The annual rainfall total should be high (above 1,000 mm) to maintain water levels in the reservoir **(1)**. Temperatures should be as low as possible to reduce the amount of water lost through evaporation **(1)**. High evaporation rates can alter the hydrological cycle, affecting the annual amount of rainfall received and thus reducing storage capacity **(1)**.   **5 marks**

Human factors might include:

Dams should be close to an urban area to provide demand and a market for water and electricity, for example Las Vegas **(1)**. They should be built in areas that are easily accessible to allow materials into the area, as well as workers **(1)**. The number of people displaced by building the dam and the loss of farmland needs to be taken into account **(1)** as well as the amount of money needed to be paid out in compensation **(1)**. Historical sites, such as the Rainbow Bridge on the Colorado River, and tribal burial grounds are at risk of being destroyed by the rising waters, which could cause distress to many people **(1)**.   **5 marks**

b) **Hint:** You should refer to a specific case study and include examples. Try to avoid a general answer as this could lose you marks.

The damming of the Omo River in Ethiopia has stopped its natural flood cycles, reducing the levels of moisture and nutrient-rich sediment that the Omo deposits each year; this affects the fertility of the soil **(1)**. The filling of the Gibe III reservoir has flooded large areas of land, destroying the natural environment and the natural habitat of animals such as the Nile crocodile **(1)**. The river flow is much reduced, forcing local tribes such as the Karo and the Mursi to move their cattle into Mago National Park, which affects the protected wildlife there **(1)**. Lake Turkana could shrink dramatically as 90 per cent of its water comes from the Omo; the water is being held back and diverted so no longer reaches the reservoir **(1)**. The dam supplies large amounts of irrigation water, however, allowing the land to become more productive, for example the establishment of sugar plantations to the west of the Omo River **(1)**. The annual flooding of the river no longer happens, so less environmental damage is done **(1)**.   **5 marks**

8 Development and Health

a) **Hint:** You should refer to a country you have studied and give examples in your answer. Your answer should reflect how the lives of the people have improved. You can answer this question as one whole question instead of in two parts, that is, give the strategy then evaluate its effectiveness.

If rural China chosen:

In rural China 'barefoot doctors' undertake basic health care, for example disease prevention, education, maternal and child health care, and collecting disease information, as well as teaching basic hygiene such as washing hands before eating and after using latrines, thus improving health in rural areas **(1)**. If illnesses are beyond their capabilities, barefoot doctors refer patients to physicians at community health centres **(1)**. In some areas, doctors visit rural villages and treat those who are too ill to travel to the nearest hospital and might otherwise die **(1)**. They run clinics in the larger villages and take a mobile health van to more remote villages. This means that the villagers are able to receive vital health care, which can reduce the death rate **(1)**. Some primary health care programmes provide villages with local dispensaries, which improves people's health by giving them access to essential modern drugs and family planning **(1)**. Some programmes also implement improvements to sanitation facilities and the provision of clean drinking water, reducing the number of cases of cholera and malaria and improving the health of the working population. This allows them to continue to work and provide for their families **(1)**.   **6 marks**

b) **Hint:** Give reasons as to why the strategy was successful or not. Since this question asks for an evaluation, you can put forward your own opinion.

Barefoot doctors are successful as they live in the community and are readily available to help those in need, thus reducing the death rate **(1)**. Teaching the use of simple hygiene is successful in reducing the spread of disease **(1)**. It also reduces the pressure on large hospitals, enabling them to deal with more serious illnesses **(1)**. The barefoot doctors are effective as they provide health care for people in more remote areas, where budgets and resources can be limited **(1)**. Training costs are low – for example in India it costs $100 to train a health worker for a year – making it accessible for developing countries **(1)**.   **4 marks**

9 Global Climate Change

a) **Hint:** Give a cause then explain how it contributes to global warming. Avoid giving a list of causes as this will achieve a limited number of marks.

The increasing demand for power causes an increase in the burning and extraction of fossil fuels, especially in newly industrialised countries such as India and China, which results in the release of carbon dioxide and other heat-trapping 'greenhouse' gases into the atmosphere **(1)**. Growing populations and the consequent rise in the use of electrical gadgets increases the demand for electricity, thus increasing the amount of carbon dioxide released into the atmosphere **(1)**. The number of private cars on the road, as well as an increase in the use of lorries to transport goods (for example through food shopping online), has increased the levels of exhaust emissions such as nitrous oxides in the atmosphere **(1)**. A growing demand for products from all over the world, and the improved accessibility of air travel through no-frills airlines such as

EasyJet and Ryanair, has led to an increased use of aircraft and, therefore, increased consumption of fossil fuels **(1)**. Clearing forests releases large amounts of carbon dioxide. Also, plants and trees use carbon dioxide to grow, so deforestation means that there are fewer trees to absorb the additional carbon dioxide, meaning that more carbon dioxide stays in the atmosphere, trapping more heat **(2)**. The growing global population means there is a greater demand for food, resulting in more cattle being farmed. Cows produce harmful gases such as methane, which contribute to global warming **(1)**.

6 marks

b) **Hint:** The question asks for discussion so you need to give reasons in your answer. Description will get you a limited number of marks. You should give both positive and negative effects in your answer. Always try to include named examples in your answer.

Global warming is causing glaciers to melt, putting millions of people at risk from floods in low-lying coastal areas such as the Fenlands of eastern England **(1)**. Warmer water temperatures affect aquatic life; Scotland's hottest year on record was in 2003 and this rise in temperature killed hundreds of adult salmon as rivers became too warm for them to extract enough oxygen from the water **(1)**. Warming sea temperatures force fish shoals to move to cooler waters, affecting catches and the livelihoods of people in the fishing industry **(1)**. In other areas in the UK, increased temperatures can result in some crops failing, such as potatoes, but at the same time can encourage the growth of soft fruits that like warmer conditions **(1)**. Longer growing seasons are possible in many areas in northern Europe and this could increase both food production and the range of crops being grown **(1)**.

4 marks

10 Trade, Aid and Geopolitics

Hint: This question can be answered in two parts or as one. In this sample answer the reasons and the impacts are given together. To show where the marks for each section come from they have been coded 'R' for reason and 'Im' for impact.

Some countries, such as the UK and USA, have the knowledge and technology to make and sell manufactured products; these sell at high prices so larger profits are made **(R/Im 1)**. These manufactured products also sell for a more stable price with few fluctuations, so countries can plan for the future with confidence in future income **(Im 1)**. Developing countries mainly trade in primary products that sell for prices that fluctuate, making it difficult to invest in development for the future **(Im 1)**. Commodity price instability has a negative impact on economic growth, countries' financial resources and income distribution, and may lead to increased poverty as many countries, especially in Africa, derive more than 90 per cent of their export earnings from commodities **(Im 1)**. Often it is the developed countries that set the price for primary products and keep them as low as possible by 'playing' developing countries against each other **(R 1)**. Some countries are too reliant on one or two low-value exports: if anything happens to the price/production of these export products, the country's economy is hit badly **(Im 1)**. World commodity prices are very unstable; they are driven by changes in global demand and supply. Developing countries are particularly affected by these changes, which can result in increased poverty and reduced public funding for health and education **(Im 1)**. Less money coming in means that many children are forced to work instead of going to school; this results in an illiterate population that is unable to access well-paid employment, with the consequent lack of opportunities and poorer quality of living for these people **(Im 1)**. The lack of well-paid jobs means that many people live in shanty town-type accommodation, with little access to clean water, safe electricity or sanitation **(Im 1)**, which causes diseases such as cholera to spread rapidly and lowers the life expectancy of people living here **(Im 1)**. Trading alliances such as the European Union can control trade terms for the benefit of their members and make it difficult for non-members to do as well **(R 1)**. For example, they can set up tariffs and import duties that they charge non-member countries, which makes goods from these countries appear less competitive **(Im 1)**. They can also set quotas that limit the amount of a product that a non-member country can sell to the member country **(R 1)**.   **10 marks**

11 Energy

a) **Hint:** The answer should refer to the changes. Do not describe the pie charts. You need to give reasons for the changes.

There is a reduction in the amount of energy generation using coal and other fossil fuels as the UK government wants to reduce the UK's carbon emissions **(1)**. Also, fossil fuels such as coal and gas are finite; gas reserves are limited and the coal that does remain is found much deeper in the ground, making it more difficult to extract **(1)**. The government wants to increase the amount of energy that comes from renewable sources, hence the increase in the percentage of renewables **(1)**. The EU has set targets for the amount of energy to come from renewable sources to try to address global warming: the 2020 target for the UK is 15 per cent **(1)**. The government gives incentives to the public and industries to save energy; for example, grants are available to help make homes more energy efficient, with some people taking up the option of installing solar panels **(1)**. Other sources, such as biomass and river power, are being introduced to increase the use of green energy and reduce the UK's carbon footprint **(1)**.   **4 marks**

b) **Hint:** Since this question is about suitability you can give both advantages and disadvantages that a country has when producing a particular type of electricity. You can talk about a variety of renewable energy types in your answer or you can go into detail on one particular type. This sample answer has examples of both. Remember, you should refer to named examples in your answer.

Hydroelectric energy involves generating electricity using the power of moving water. Electricity is generated by the force of water turning turbines, so steep slopes, ideally mountain areas, are needed **(1)**. Glaciated areas with hanging valleys in Scotland are suitable as they provide the drop necessary to turn the turbines to provide electricity **(1)**. A high average rainfall is also essential so that the reservoirs needed to store the water are always full, for example Foyers on the shores of Loch Ness **(1)**. The rock needs to be impermeable to prevent loss of water through seepage **(1)**. In the UK most suitable sites for hydroelectric power stations are already used, so there is very little scope to increase the use of hydroelectric power in the future **(1)**.

Solar power is suitable in areas where there are long hours of sunshine to power solar panels. It is more suitable in Mediterranean regions, for example Mallorca, than Scotland, where sunshine hours are more limited **(1)**.

Geothermal power is suitable in areas of volcanic activity, for example Iceland, where the geothermal energy from the Earth's core is used to generate electricity and heat houses **(1)**. Japan, one of world's most seismically active nations, has recently been investing in geothermal power and generates as much as 23 million kilowatts of energy a year. This makes it less dependent on other nations for fuel **(1)**.

Wind power is most efficient in areas with no barriers to the force of the wind, ensuring a continual supply of power to the turbines **(1)**. Wind power can be controversial, however, as it causes visual pollution as well as disturbing local habitats **(1)**. Wind power is dependent on the continual supply of wind. As it is difficult to store the energy produced, there are problems with providing energy on calm days **(1)**.

The generation of electricity from wave power is currently under development. As wave energy is distributed across the globe, it may offer many countries the benefit of security of supply **(1)**.

Biofuels (the burning of plant matter to produce energy) can provide continuous, affordable energy in developing countries **(1)**. The disadvantage is that burning plant material causes air pollution and makes less land available for crop production to supply the growing populations of developing countries **(1)**. **6 marks**

Section 4: Application of Geographical Skills

12 **Hint:** This scenario question is designed to examine your geographical skills, including interpreting an Ordnance Survey map, using six-figure grid references and understanding/using scale, direction and distance. You should also be able to extract and interpret information from a variety of graphs and charts. In this question you will be able to demonstrate to the examiner the geographical skills you have learned and developed throughout your Higher course. You should use/evaluate the information you have been given to make judgements and back up your answer with map evidence and information from the diagrams. This question is worth 10 marks.

Hydroelectric schemes need large, deep areas for the reservoirs and housing equipment. The proposed sites in this scheme have already been excavated as they were previously used as slate quarries, as shown in Diagram Q12A, so they will save on the cost of excavation **(1)**. A large drop in height is also needed to allow a fast flow of water to generate the electricity. Cefn Du is around 400 m, while the lower quarry is around 200 m, so a suitable height difference is found here – around 200 m **(1)**. Since hydroelectricity is created using water, a continuous amount of rainfall is needed to ensure that the reservoirs remain full. This is the case here, as can be seen in Diagram Q12B: the area is seen to have rainfall all year round with a peak in winter **(1)**. Looking at Diagram Q12B it can also be seen that temperatures throughout the year are low, even in summer (the maximum temperature in Llanberis is only 12 °C in July and August). This means that little water should be lost through evaporation **(1)**. The map shows lots of disused quarries, for example at 564604, and waste tips, for example at 554602, and, as the photograph in Diagram Q12A shows, this makes the area look unattractive. Perhaps an HEP scheme is a better use of this derelict land and will improve the scenery of the area **(1)**. This scheme will generate green electricity as it uses the natural resources of the area – in this case water – thus reducing the country's carbon footprint as well as reducing the need to use fossil fuels to produce electricity in coal-fired power stations. This point is confirmed by the developer in Diagram Q12E **(1)**.

However, there are some disadvantages. Looking at the map it can be seen that there is only one main transport route in the area – the A4086. There are only a few minor roads on the outskirts of Llanberis and no roads leading to the proposed sites, meaning that roads would need to be constructed. This will result in the local environment being disturbed, as well as subjecting the local population to noise and air pollution **(1)**. Large lorries and additional traffic would be forced to travel through Llanberis during construction, causing traffic congestion on the small roads as well as increasing the risk of accidents in the area **(1)**. This area is very popular with tourists as can be seen in Diagram Q12C. Up to 4.27 million people visit each year, especially to access Snowdonia; congested roads may put visitors off **(1)**. This could adversely affect the prosperity and standard of living of the local population; as Diagram Q12C shows, visitors spend around £396 million each year in businesses such as the museum at 584603 and the hotel at 583598 **(1)**. The location of this development is in an area of natural beauty, as well as an area that tourists use to access Snowdonia. Access to the area would be restricted during the construction work, and the scenery would be spoiled by a huge concrete dam **(1)**. It may be necessary to transfer the electricity using pylons and, again, these would interrupt the scenery; cables could be put underground or the pylons put below eye level, however **(1)**.

In my opinion it would be a good idea to go ahead with this project. I feel that the scenery would not be spoiled as the photograph in Diagram Q12A shows the area to be unsightly; the new buildings and reservoirs would actually improve the scenic ambience of the area **(1)**. In some cases HEP stations attract visitors, for example Cruachan in Argyle and Bute, so it could in fact bring money into the area, increasing the prosperity of the local population **(1)**. The area is full of waste tips and derelict quarries so this would be a better and more productive use of the land. It may also bring jobs into the area during the construction stage, as well as maintaining the scheme when it is up and running **(1)**. The production of green electricity will help the government to meet its target of using less fossil fuel to reduce the effects of global warming **(1)**.

Practice Paper B

Section 1: Physical Environments

1   **Hint:** Name a factor then explain its effect on the hydrograph. Avoid listing factors. Avoid description as this will gain few marks.

The size of the drainage basin has an effect; large basins will have high peak discharges because they catch more precipitation **(1)**. Larger basins have longer lag times than small basins because the water takes longer to reach the rivers **(1)**. Basins with steep slopes will have a high peak discharge and a short lag time because the water can travel faster downhill **(1)**. Permeable rocks and soils, for example sandy soils, absorb water easily; this allows water to travel slowly through the soil, reducing peak discharge and increasing the lag time in a river **(1)**. Impermeable soils, for example clay soils, are more closely packed; as water cannot infiltrate the soil it reaches the river more quickly, reducing the lag time **(1)**. Vegetation slows the movement of water into river channels as it intercepts precipitation, which increases lag time **(1)**. The removal of natural vegetation and replacement with impermeable concrete/hard surfaces and drains can speed up overland flow and can lead to higher river levels **(1)**. Water is also lost due to evaporation and transpiration from vegetation, which reduces the peak discharge of a river **(1)**.   **5 marks**

2   **Hint:** A well-labelled sequence of diagrams could gain full marks. The question asks for a diagram so if you do not include one in your answer you could lose a mark.

If terminal moraine chosen:

Moraine is material carried along by a glacier; it is made up of debris accumulated by plucking and abrasion, and is pushed along by the front of the glacier **(1)**. When the glacier reaches lower altitudes or temperatures rise, the ice melts and deposits moraine at its snout **(1)**. The glacier is still moving so material is constantly added to the terminal moraine and the longer the ice melts at the same location the higher the terminal moraine **(1)**. Terminal moraine marks the furthest extent of the glacier. It forms a jumbled mass of unsorted materials that stretches across the valley floor **(1)**. Once the ice has retreated, the terminal moraine can often form a natural dam, creating a ribbon lake **(1)**.   **5 marks**

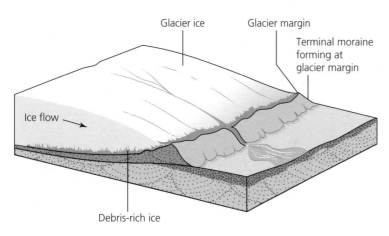

If drumlin chosen:

Drumlins are elongated hills of glacial deposits and are formed when the ice is still moving **(1)**. The steep slope faces upstream and the lee slope is the gentler, longer axis of the drumlin, which indicates the direction in which the glacier was moving **(1)**. The drumlin would have been deposited when the glacier became overloaded with sediment; the material was deposited as the glacier lost power due to melting **(1)**. It is possible that there was a small obstacle in the ground that caused the till to build up around it forming the drumlin **(1)**. It may also have been reshaped by further ice movements after it was deposited **(1)**.   **5 marks**

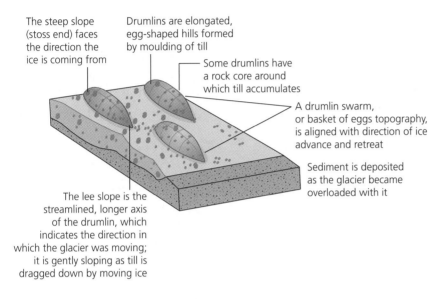

The steep slope (stoss end) faces the direction the ice is coming from

Drumlins are elongated, egg-shaped hills formed by moulding of till

Some drumlins have a rock core around which till accumulates

A drumlin swarm, or basket of eggs topography, is aligned with direction of ice advance and retreat

Sediment is deposited as the glacier became overloaded with it

The lee slope is the streamlined, longer axis of the drumlin, which indicates the direction in which the glacier was moving; it is gently sloping as till is dragged down by moving ice

If esker chosen:

Eskers are mounds of sand and gravel that snake their way across the landscape and are produced as a result of running water in, on or under a glacier **(1)**. When the glacier retreats the sediment that had been deposited in the channel is lowered to the land surface where it forms a mound, or hill, that is roughly parallel to the path of the original glacial river **(1)**. The water is unable to escape sideways because of the restricting walls of ice **(1)** and the stream bed is gradually built up above the level of the ground on which the glacier rests **(1)**. The ice that formed the sides and roof of the tunnel later disappears, leaving behind sand and gravel deposits in ridges with long and twisting shapes **(1)**.   **5 marks**

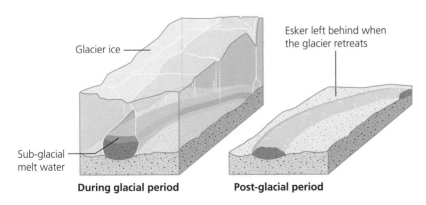

Glacier ice

Esker left behind when the glacier retreats

Sub-glacial melt water

During glacial period   **Post-glacial period**

3 **Hint:** The question asks for comparison and explanation, so avoid simple description. Make sure you give a reason for each point you make. You should comment on precipitation totals (the number of rainy days) as well as seasonal distribution. You could enhance your answer by using statistics.

Gao has 200 mm of rainfall compared to Bobo-Dioulasso with 1,000 mm. Bobo-Dioulasso has a peak in August, whereas there is a higher peak June in Abidjan **(1)**. Gao has a distinct dry season from October to May with one peak, whereas Abidjan has year-round rainfall with two peaks: one in June and the other in October **(1)**.

Abidjan sits south of the ITCZ and is influenced by hot, humid maritime tropical air from the Gulf of Guinea for most of the year **(1)**. The twin precipitation peaks can be attributed to the ITCZ moving northwards in the early part of the year and then southwards later in the year in line with the thermal equator/overhead Sun **(1)**. Gao, on the other hand, is under the influence of hot, dry continental tropical air blowing from the Sahara and lies well to the north of the ITCZ for most of the year **(1)**. Bobo-Dioulasso is in an 'in-between' position, getting more rainy days and heavy summer precipitation from June to September when the ITCZ is furthest north **(1)**. **5 marks**

Section 2: Human Environments

4 **Hint:** Avoid giving generalised answers. You should refer to a specific case study. For full marks you must explain both positive and negative points. Avoid giving the same point in reverse – this takes time away from answering other questions and will gain you no marks.

If migration from Poland to the UK chosen:

Positive impacts (for the UK as the receiving country): Polish migrants are prepared to do menial, unskilled, low-paid jobs in factories, catering, cleaning and labouring that many UK citizens do not want to do **(1)**. Polish workers are prepared to work long, unsociable hours and for less money than a British worker **(1)**. Job vacancies in the UK and the skills gap can be filled by skilled Polish migrants, for example managerial and professional vacancies **(1)**. Polish migrants pay National Insurance contributions, which have helped the UK to cope with supporting its ageing population **(1)**. Migrants bring energy and new ideas; the culture of the UK is enhanced by the migrants with new foods, fashion and festivals **(1)**.

Negative impacts (for the UK as the receiving country): Tensions can occur with the local population in relation to housing, benefits and health care, for example in Boston, Lincolnshire, where protests have been made to the local council **(1)**. Migrant workers are often exploited by unscrupulous employers, with gang masters supplying a labour force for much less than the minimum wage **(1)**. Many immigrants cannot find a job so claim benefits, putting pressure on the finances of the UK government as well as pressure on local authorities to supply education and health care for additional people **(1)**.   **5 marks**

5 **Hint:** Avoid simple description. Do not list the strategies as this will gain few marks. Name the strategy then explain its purpose.

If rainforest chosen:

Afforestation and reforestation programmes – such as the World Bank's Amazon Region Protected Programme – where trees are planted in new areas or replanted in felled areas, aim to conserve soils or protect existing forest **(1)**. Companies that operate in ways that minimise damage to the environment are encouraged. They might agree to replace the trees as well as to help the region financially **(1)**. National parks and reserves are areas created by the government and protected by law. These laws prevent or reduce the harm caused to the area by commercial developments **(1)**. Ecotourism is popular within these national parks and reserves, and the money generated by tourism is reinvested in the area **(1)**. Education can be used to teach people about the importance of the environment, and the global and local effects of deforestation, and use this to help save rainforests **(1)**. Save The Rainforest, Inc. offers educational tours and student trips to tropical rainforest destinations in Belize, Costa Rica, Galapagos and Panama, which raise awareness of the importance of rainforests **(1)**.

If semi-arid area chosen:

Moveable fencing allows farmers to restrict grazing animals to a particular area, allowing the remaining land to recover and reduce overgrazing **(1)**. Contour ploughing, where slopes are ploughed following the contour lines, slows water run-off, allowing it to penetrate into the soil and prevent soil erosion **(1)**. Terraces can be cut into the hillside to slow water run-off, especially irrigation water **(1)**. Lines of stones laid along the contour lines called 'magic stones' catch the rain water and allow it to percolate into the soil, keeping it moist and stopping it from being washed away **(1)**. Trees planted in rows act as shelter belts, preventing the wind from drying out the soil and blowing it away; the roots also help to bind the soil together **(1)**. The use of irrigation, that is the artificial watering of crops, keeps the soil moist as well as the plants, preventing the soil from being blown away **(1)**.   **6 marks**

6   **Hint**: Avoid generalised answers. You should mention specific examples in your answer.

If Rocinha Shanty Town, Brazil, chosen:

Self-help schemes have been implemented, where residents are provided with materials and given training and tools to improve their houses, for example replacing wooden shacks with brick and tile buildings **(1)**. The local authority is committed to spending £200 million to replace wooden buildings or those on dangerously steep slopes with newer, larger houses that will reduce overcrowding and the risk of lives lost from landslides **(1)**. Electricity, along with mains water, has been introduced; this improves living conditions and general health by allowing access to cookers and fridges to keep food fresh; mains water reduces the spread of disease from dirty well water **(1)**. Roads have been paved, allowing health workers and goods to be transported through the shanty town **(1)**, and streets have been widened to allow access to emergency vehicles and waste collection vehicles, helping to reduce the spread of disease **(1)**. The government is looking at rural investment; this involves improving the quality of life in rural areas to encourage people to stay instead of migrating to urban areas and increasing the spread of shanty towns **(1)**.   **4 marks**

Section 3: Global Issues

7   River Basin Management

a)   **Hint:** Avoid simple description. You need to give reasons why water management is needed. Use the facts and figures in the diagrams to support your answer.

High rainfall in April, May and June means that flooding is a threat. Dams such as Garrison are needed to combat the threat of flooding **(1)**. The population growth predicted for the future in the Missouri basin means that demand for water from the growing population will be high; increased demand for domestic and drinking water means that water management is required **(1)**. Around 25 per cent of all the agricultural land in the USA lies in the Missouri basin, so water management is important for irrigation purposes **(1)**. The river has many tributaries, causing river levels to rise dangerously, especially with the spring snowmelt; water management is essential to prevent flooding **(1)**. In recent years temperatures have been above average in some areas of the basin in the summer months; as drought is likely, water control is needed so that water stored in the spring can be used to irrigate the land in summer **(1)**.   **5 marks**

b)   **Hint:** For full marks you must mention both people and environment. You will get no marks for mentioning negative impacts. Avoid general answers – for full marks you must refer to a specific water scheme you have studied, putting in examples.

If the Missouri chosen:

Control of the river, through the construction of levees along the lower river and major tributaries, channelisation of floodplain tributaries, and an extensive reservoir system in the large tributary basins of the Platte, Kansas and Osage Rivers, stopped flooding in many areas. This resulted in fewer people being displaced and fewer injuries/deaths **(1)**. The six main dams and their reservoirs can store three years' worth of rainfall, removing the threat of drought and thus ensuring a constant supply of water for domestic requirements and irrigation **(1)**. This means there is more food available for consumption and for sale, which improves the health of the people and the economy of the country **(1)**. The cheap supply of hydroelectric power encourages industry into the area, creating jobs and improving the standard of living there **(1)**. The reservoirs encourage tourists into the area, improving the local economy: the Missouri reservoirs contribute around $100 million to the regional economy each year **(1)**. Improved facilities, such as boat ramps and campgrounds, were built, improving leisure facilities for locals as well as tourists **(1)**. The reservoirs encourage new wildlife into the region through the creation of a new water-bird habitat and spawning areas for fish, allowing the local population to enjoy the natural environment **(1)**.   **5 marks**

8   Development and Health

Hint: This question can be answered in two parts or as a combined answer, as shown below. To show where the marks for each section come from they have been coded 'C' for efforts to combat disease and 'E' for evaluation of effectiveness. For full marks, both efforts to combat the disease and evaluate their effectiveness must be mentioned.

If malaria chosen:

Drugs such as chloroquine can be given to people to stop them catching malaria or to treat malaria sufferers. Malarone is a newer drug and is safe for children **(C 1)**. Chloroquine is cheap to produce but in recent years the mosquitoes have become immune to it, so it is less effective. It needs to be taken properly to be effective and can be too expensive for poor people in countries like Malawi **(E 1)**. Malarone has proved to be effective and has few side effects, so it has the potential to do well **(E 1)**. Vaccines against malaria have been developed but they are still at the trial stage in places like Columbia and Gambia **(C 1)**. Vaccines can be administered through primary health care schemes and, if given to children, would reduce the incidence of malaria and reduce infant mortality rates in many areas **(C 1)**. Educating people is an effective, simple and cheap way of combating malaria and can be done through primary health care schemes using songs/drama. Advice includes using bed nets, covering the skin to prevent bites and using screen doors and windows to stop mosquitoes entering the house **(C 1)**. Bed nets are relatively cheap and stop people getting bitten, reducing the chance of catching malaria **(E 1)**. Visitors and locals can also take antimalarial drugs, but they are expensive and have to be taken regularly to be effective **(E 1)**. Draining areas of stagnant water, such as puddles and swamps, reduces areas where the mosquitoes breed. However, there can be heavy rainfall every day in tropical areas, so new areas of stagnant water appear all the time; having to drain the area constantly is time-consuming as it needs to be done every day **(C/E 1)**. Breeding areas and homes can be sprayed with insecticides such as DDT, which kills the mosquitoes and their larvae. This is effective if done carefully, but over time the mosquitoes have become immune; DDT is also harmful to the environment and is now banned in some countries **(C/E 1)**. Egg whites can be sprayed on stagnant water to suffocate the larvae (it clogs up their breathing tubes so that they drown). This works but, in areas where food is scarce, it is a waste of a valuable food source **(C/E 1)**.   **10 marks**

9   **Global Climate Change**

   a)   **Hint:** Avoid description and lists. Make sure you explain your answer.

   People can reduce their use of fossil fuels such as coal, oil and natural gases by switching to renewable energy sources such as hydroelectric power, wind power and solar power **(1)**. People can be encouraged to walk, car share, use public transport and cycle to work to reduce the number of vehicles on the road; this reduces the amount of greenhouse gases being released in the atmosphere **(1)**. People can use lead-free petrol, as well as modified engines with catalytic converters, to reduce pollution into the atmosphere **(1)**. Laws can be introduced to reduce the burning of the rainforest: trees store carbon and release carbon dioxide into the atmosphere when they are burnt **(1)**. Replanting schemes can be introduced where forests have been destroyed to ensure that carbon dioxide is recycled by the forest, reducing the build-up of greenhouse gases **(1)**. In the UK, there are strict laws for the disposal of fridges and other appliances that contain CFC gases; this ensures they are disposed of safely instead of being dumped in landfill where the gases can escape **(1)**.   **6 marks**

   b)   **Hint:** This question asks for evaluation so you need to assess how well the strategies have worked. You can comment on positive and negative aspects of the strategy. Try to give figures or use examples in your answer.

In the UK the introduction of targets has been partly successful as more green energy is being used and produced, but at the moment it looks like the 15 per cent target set by the government might not be reached. The planned use of offshore wind farms has proved too expensive and some may be abandoned **(1)**. Public transport has been improved to encourage people to leave cars at home. This has been partly successful as more people now use public transport, but some people still prefer to have the freedom to travel by car **(1)**. The car industry has been working to produce new fuel-efficient engines with reduced emissions. This has been successful, as more eco-cars are now on the road; some have engines that shut down when stationary, thus reducing their carbon dioxide emissions **(1)**. Many developed countries still do not pay developing countries a reasonable price for the goods that they produce, so countries like Brazil still continue to cut down the rainforest, which decreases the store of carbon in the trees, thus adversely affecting the amount of carbon dioxide in the atmosphere **(1)**.   **4 marks**

10 Trade, Aid and Geopolitics

a) **Hint:** Avoid simple descriptive answers. You must refer to the impact that this type of trade has on the people and the country.

Developing countries receive less money for trade, which means that they have fewer well-paid jobs, forcing people to live in poor accommodation such as shanty towns with limited access to clean water, sanitation and electricity **(1)**. Diseases such as cholera can spread rapidly in this environment, resulting in poor health and shorter life expectancy **(1)**. Children are unable to access education; instead they have to work to provide an income for their family, resulting in a poorly educated population with little access to well-paid jobs **(1)**. Poorly paid jobs, lack of education and disease mean that people struggle to survive from day to day. This results in a cycle of poverty, perpetuating this state in the next generation **(1)**. Multinational companies move into developing countries providing jobs for the people but paying the lowest wages possible as they want to manufacture products at the cheapest price. As a result, the local population continues to live in poverty **(1)**. In the developed world, many industries are supported by their governments in the form of grants and subsidies, meaning they can sell their products at a very competitive price, undercutting industries in the developing world and causing them to lose money **(1)**. Wealthier developed nations can form trading alliances, such as the EU; these alliances can use tariffs to stop goods coming into the region at a cheaper price. Developing countries make less profit because of the tariffs and therefore have less money with which to fund development **(1)**.   **6 marks**

b) **Hint:** Avoid a simple list of strategies. You should explain the strategy and give examples in your answer. To help you revise, an answer for the impact of the strategies is also included.

Many developing countries took out large loans to help them develop their industries but ended up in debt when they tried to repay the loans. This debt continued to increase, making it impossible for them to develop trade and industry. Some developed countries came up with debt cancellation in which some or all of a country's debt was cancelled **(1)**. For example, the Jubilee 2000 campaign was a coalition of 40 countries whose aim was to get rid of $90 billion in debt owed by the world's poorest countries to some of the world's richest countries and international banks **(1)**. Debt cancellation enables governments in poor countries to increase key public spending in areas such as health and education, which in turn helps the country to develop **(1)**. In a conservation swap, part of a country's debt is paid off in exchange for investment in conservation – many poorer countries have abundant natural resources that they exploit as they are poor and in debt **(1)**. Part of the rainforest in Guatemala has been protected by a conservation swap **(1)**. The Fairtrade Foundation was established in the UK to try to develop a fairer trading system. Fair trade means that the producer receives a guaranteed and fair price for their product regardless of the price on the world market **(1)**. This means that producers' quality of life should improve, alongside the long-term prospects for their children **(1)**. **4 marks**

Sample answer considering the impact of such strategies:

Zambia had $4 million of debt cancelled; one year later the country had enough money to start a free health care scheme for millions of people in rural areas – a dramatic improvement in their quality of life **(1)**. Despite successful debt abolition campaigns, World Bank figures show that external debts owed by developing countries are still increasing; they owe around $4 trillion in total **(1)**. As a result of the Jubilee 2000 campaign, the UK government cancelled much but not all of the debts owed to it by poorer nations **(1)**; many banks have not cancelled debts, however, and many countries all over the world still suffer the effects of debt **(1)**. Fair trade is now an international movement and its influence continues to grow. More than 4,500 products bear the fair trade mark and 72 per cent of the UK population recognises the fair trade logo **(1)**. In addition, more than 7 million people in Africa, Asia and South America benefit from fair trade, including farmers, farm workers and their families **(1)**. However, for millions of workers on farms and in factories, access to a living wage continues to be out of reach **(1)**. **4 marks**

11 Energy

a) **Hint:** Read the question carefully as this particular question can ask for either developed countries or developing countries, or both. In this instance you will not get marks for talking about both and will use up valuable time that could be used for other questions. The answer below is a combined answer covering both developed and developing countries.

The world's population is growing constantly and is predicted to increase by 25 per cent in the next 20 years. This will increase the demand for energy in both developed and developing countries **(1)**. The majority of the increase will be in developing countries such as China and India, as they require energy to continue to develop their economies **(1)**. Rising energy demands from economic output and improved standards of living will put added pressure on the energy supply **(1)**. The high standards of living in the developed countries are attributable to high energy consumption levels, with widespread use of expensive consumer goods and the expansion of IT **(1)**. In developing countries, an increase in standards of living means an increase in the demand for energy to power televisions, washing machines, fridge freezers, air conditioning and so on **(1)**. Countries such as China are developing manufacturing industries that use up enormous amounts of energy **(1)**. Developing countries increasingly trade bulky primary products with developed countries; these goods need to be transported around the world, using up more fossil fuels **(1)**. In countries such as India, car ownership is becoming more common due to an increased standard of living, so more energy is needed to run these vehicles **(1)**. The energy increase in developed countries is smaller because, although the population is growing, it is growing much more slowly. In cases like Germany, the death rate is higher than the birth rate **(1)**. Developed countries are being encouraged to conserve energy to reduce the effects of global warming, so energy consumption is growing much more slowly **(1)**.   **6 marks**

b) **Hint:** Read the question carefully. It can ask for a developed country, developing country or both, and refer to either renewable or non-renewable energy. You will only gain marks for the specific topic asked.

If HEP chosen:

Hydroelectric power harnesses a free resource, which is sustainable for the future **(1)**. Electricity can be produced at a constant rate and, if electricity is not needed, the sluice gates can be shut, stopping electricity generation **(1)**. The water can be saved for use another time when electricity demand is high **(1)**. Dams are designed to last many decades so can contribute to the generation of electricity for many years to come **(1)**. When in use, the electricity produced by dam systems does not produce greenhouse gases, so does not pollute the atmosphere **(1)**. Hydroelectricity does not 'use up' water – all of the water is returned to its source of origin, thus it is a clean source of energy **(1)**.   **4 marks**

Section 4: Application of Geographical Skills

12 **Hint:** You will be given a set of conditions to follow. This scenario question is worth 10 marks. It is designed to examine your geographical skills, including interpreting an Ordnance Survey map, using six-figure grid references and understanding/using scale, direction and distance. You should also be able to extract and interpret information from a variety of graphs and charts. In this question you will be able to demonstrate to the examiner the geographical skills you have learned and developed throughout your Higher course. These should be used to help you answer the question. You should use/evaluate the information you have been given to make judgements and back up your answer with map evidence and information from the diagrams.

One advantage of this proposal is that there is a large amount of empty land available to accommodate this small development. The contour lines on Diagram Q12 also show the land to be relatively flat, and so easy to build on **(1)**. Although the land is Forestry Commission land, as identified on Diagram Q12 and the Ordnance Survey map, it is available for release for housing as the National Park Development Plan has identified a need for social housing **(1)**. The B837 road passes the proposed site, so transport of goods in and out of the site should be easy; this road provides good access to the site and surrounding area **(1)**. The site is close to the hamlet of Balmaha so residents of the new housing would be able to access the local amenities such as fishing and boating (grid reference 419909), as well as enjoying the beautiful views and scenery of the area **(1)**. The West Highland Way passes close by the proposed site, as shown on Diagram Q12, so the path would be accessible from the new development and might attract new buyers into the area, thus supporting the local economy **(1)**. The housing will provide affordable accommodation for the original population, as stated by James Fraser in Diagram Q12D, and may stop depopulation. Young people might choose to stay in the area if there is suitable, affordable housing available **(1)**. This might also allow businesses in the area to attract workers; they may have struggled in the past if it was difficult to recruit workers because there was no suitable housing available **(1)**. The housing as described in Diagram Q12A will be designed using environmentally friendly materials that blend into the area to preserve the scenic views in the National Park and not detract from its beauty and appeal to tourists **(1)**.

However, this housing will be built on Forestry Commission land, which is the habitat of many different types of wildlife, as stated in Diagram Q12C; some of these are rare, including red squirrels and slow-worms. The removal of trees could further endanger their existence, as well as adding to global warming **(1)**. The West Highland Way is one of the main attractions for tourists coming to Scotland and, as can be seen on the Ordnance Survey map, it runs close by the site. The new housing could detract from the scenery, affecting the tourist trade that many businesses in or near Balmaha depend on for their livelihood, for example the Oak Tree Inn **(1)**. Balmaha is a small hamlet and this new housing will increase the population of the area greatly, putting pressure on local amenities as well as causing more congestion on the narrow country roads, and increasing the carbon footprint of the area **(1)**.

Having looked at the Ordnance Survey map and the sources I think that this housing should go ahead. There is a lack of any type of new accommodation in the Balmaha area and the new housing should be built to meet this demand. The accommodation will meet the demands of the rental market as well as offering the possibility of two private plots **(1)**.

People brought up in the area may not be able to find affordable accommodation; what is available may be too dear for them and instead be bought up by wealthy people from outside the area. As a result of this, young people leave the area, causing depopulation. This new housing will give the young people of the area a chance to stay here **(1)**. Although this building project is within the National Park, where development is restricted by law, the needs of the people who live within the Park need to be considered, and the Park Authorities have identified a need for more housing. Looking at Diagram Q12A, it is to be built sympathetically and designed to blend in with the natural area **(1)**. The scenery along the West Highland Way should not be compromised as the houses will be hidden behind a screen of trees, therefore having little effect on the tourist trade **(1)**. Businesses in Balmaha may also gain from the building of these houses: the attraction of having accommodation available may attract new workers into the area **(1)**.

Practice Paper C

Section 1: Physical Environments

1 **Hint:** Avoid simple description of the soil profile. You need to explain the features of the profile. Remember that a well-labelled diagram with explanations can get full marks. This question asks for a diagram so you will lose marks if you do not use one in your answer.

Podzols tend to form on the upper slopes of upland areas where precipitation is heavy, the temperature cold, or where the vegetation is coniferous forest **(1)**. Coniferous needles produce a thin, acidic humus due to slow decomposition in a cold climate **(1)**. The ash/grey colour of the A-horizon is due to greater rainfall and lack of organic material **(1)**. Rainfall is greater than evaporation, resulting in downward leaching of the minerals **(1)**. An iron pan develops in the illuviation zone in the upper B-horizon as a result of the redeposition of iron; this can impede drainage, resulting in waterlogging and gleying in the B-horizon **(1)**. The C-horizon parent material is generally of weathered glacial material with a mixture of particle sizes and shapes **(1)**. The acid conditions are a deterrent to soil organisms such as worms; as a result the soil is not well mixed, so distinctive horizons are formed **(1)**. The slow rate of weathering of the parent rock gives a shallow soil which, due to its acidity and lack of humus, is usually infertile **(1)**.   **5 marks**

2 **Hint:** A well-labelled sequence of diagrams could gain full marks. Explaining processes in detail can gain marks. Avoid descriptive answers as these will gain you limited marks.

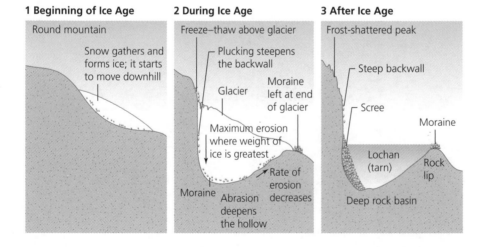

Snow accumulates in mountain hollows when more snow falls in winter than melts in the summer. North/north-east-facing slopes are more shaded so snow lies longer, with accumulated snow compressed into neve and, eventually, ice **(1)**. Plucking – when ice freezes onto bedrock, pulling loose rocks away from the backwall – makes the backwall steeper **(1)**. Abrasion occurs at the bottom of the hollow when the angular rock embedded in the ice grinds the hollow, smoothing it and making it deeper **(1)**. Frost-shattering continues to steepen the sides of the hollow as water in cracks in the rock turns to ice when temperatures drop below freezing; expansion and contraction weakens the rock until fragments break off **(1)**. Rotational sliding further deepens the central part of the hollow floor as gravity causes the ice to move **(1)**. Friction causes the ice to slow down at the front edge of the corrie, allowing a rock lip to form, which traps water as ice melts, leaving a lochan or tarn **(1)**. Thawing takes place during spring/summer, allowing water to penetrate cracks in the rocks at the base of the hollow **(1)**. The broken fragments build up over time and are removed by meltwater, further enlarging the hollow **(1)**. Frost-shattering on the backwall supplies further abrasion material as loose scree falls down the bergschrund **(1)**. This is a large crevasse separating moving ice from the ice still attached to the backwall **(1)**. As the glacier moves out of the hollow, it loses some energy and material is deposited, forming a rock lip **(1)**. As the ice retreats and melts, a deep armchair-shaped hollow is left behind **(1)**.

5 marks

3   **Hint**: You must refer to a named area in your answer. The more detail in your answer, the more marks you could achieve. You can mention different types of land-use conflict in your chosen area. This question asks for environmental conflicts, so talking about social or economic conflicts will gain you no marks and waste valuable time.

If Loch Lomond chosen:

Many tourists use a car to get to Loch Lomond then park illegally on grass verges, leading to soil erosion and destruction of plant habitat **(1)**. Traffic congestion occurs due to the sheer volume of cars visiting the area, for example around Balloch and Loch Lomond Shores, which leads to higher levels of noise and air pollution, which affect the wildlife habitat and rivers **(1)**. Some tourists leave litter behind, which looks unsightly and ruins the scenery in the area; it can also affect wildlife if they eat it **(1)**. Barbeques and camp fires beside the loch can leave scorch marks, destroying the plant and animal habitat **(1)**. Speedboats and jet skis produce large wakes (waves) behind them, which can cause erosion of the banks of the loch, while oil and diesel spills from boats pollute the water and the environment **(1)**. Hiking boots and mountain bikes cause footpath erosion on hills such as Ben A'an. In places where the path is in poor condition walkers start to walk around the edges, or avoid the built path altogether, resulting in a wider path with multiple routes; this widening of the path reduces the quality of the surrounding habitat **(1)**. Logging scars the landscape and makes it look unsightly. Growing non-native trees in rows or lines looks out of place here and destroys the natural beauty of the area **(1)**.

5 marks

Section 2: Human Environments

4 **Hint:** In this question you can give both positive and negative factors. Avoid description of the changes as this will not gain you marks. You need to discuss the consequences of the changes.

There will be an increase in the economically active population, generating more taxation money for the government **(1)**. The large workforce may encourage multinational companies to locate in India, raising the income of some people **(1)**. The population is now healthier, providing a fitter and more productive workforce **(1)**. The population is rising, which will increase demand for public services such as schools, hospitals and sanitation **(1)**. Pressure on resources such as land, building materials and fuel will also grow, leading to an increase in deforestation and pollution **(1)**. A growing population leads to an increased demand for food, which may lead to food shortages and dependency on foreign aid **(1)**. Food shortages and lack of provision of public services could lead to malnutrition and the spread of disease **(1)**. Lack of jobs in the countryside encourages rural–urban migration, which leads to the growth of shanty towns **(1)**.   **5 marks**

5 **Hint:** A simple description of the strategies will gain you no marks. You must evaluate the good points and bad points of the strategies.

If rainforest chosen:

Agroforestry – when crops are grown between trees – has been successful as the land is more productive and more sustainable than forestry or agriculture on their own **(1)**. It improves the soil fertility, and growing different crops throughout the year increases the farmer's income and food supply **(1)**. Afforestation has meant that new areas of forest have been created, but if a particular species of tree is planted, for example mahogany, it can result in a loss of biodiversity as the original conditions for growth have changed **(1)**. National Parks give some protection to an area but many poor countries do not have the resources to enforce them – illegal logging still results in the destruction of large areas of forest **(1)**. As many tropical countries are poor, they give private companies the rights to remove timber but, since they do not own the land, the companies are not willing to invest in long-term management of the land, which results in degradation **(1)**.   **5 marks**

If semi-arid area chosen:

Moveable fences are successful and allow areas of land to recover, but fencing is sometimes not available or too expensive **(1)**. Since grazing areas are used by lots of different herders arguments can occur; if an area has been fenced off there may be no grazing area available to other herders, and animals can perish **(1)**. Contour farming is effective on moderate slopes but is around 40 per cent less effective on steeper slopes **(1)**. Terraces are successful as they slow the water flow, allowing more water to be absorbed, which keeps the soil moist and prevents it from being blown/washed away. However, maintaining the terraces is very labour-intensive **(1)**. Magic stones are effective as they have no financial implication and can increase crop yields by over 50 per cent **(1)**. Shelter belts reduce the effects of sand storms and the effects of temperature, create more favourable conditions for plant growth and increase production **(1)**. Irrigation is successful as it allows crops to grow in periods of drought; if used on a regular basis, however, it can make the soil saline, resulting in the need for fertilisers that poor farmers cannot afford **(1)**.   **5 marks**

6 **Hint:** Do not list or use simple description of the housing. You must give reasons for the need for housing management. You need to name a city then give actual examples from your chosen city.

If Glasgow chosen:

Much of Glasgow's housing was old tenements (multi-occupancy buildings) built during the nineteenth century to house the growing population. By the 1950s it had deteriorated into unsafe, unhealthy slums, leaving Glasgow with major housing problems **(1)**. The overcrowded, unsanitary and damp conditions caused disease to spread, resulting in life expectancy in the Gorbals being around 50 years **(1)**. New council estates such as Easterhouse were built on the edge of the city to tackle the problem but they did not meet the needs of the people. There were few amenities, no work places, and destroyed community spirit, resulting in the new estates becoming abandoned and run-down **(1)**. The lack of employment and amenities led to a gang culture and crime rates rose dramatically **(1)**. High-rise flats like the Red Road Flats in Diagram Q6 were built in the 1960s, but the poor construction created similar problems to those in the new council estates. Many families chose to leave, resulting in the empty flats attracting criminals, drug dealers and squatters **(1)**.   **5 marks**

C

Section 3: Global Issues

7 River Basin Management

a) **Hint:** For full marks you need to mention all three sites. Try to avoid making reverse points, for example the feature of impermeable rock is the opposite of permeable rock. You should give the advantages and disadvantages of each site.

Site A has impermeable rock, so rain water will not soak into the ground but will run into the rivers and streams, increasing the volume of water available to be stored **(1)**. The drainage basin has many tributaries that run into the river, so a large volume of water will be available to be stored by the dam **(1)**. It lies further upstream from the urbanised area so will not cause visual pollution, and it would control the flow of water before it reaches the urbanised area, reducing the risk of flooding **(1)**.

Site B has permeable rock, so water could seep away and reduce the amount of water for storage **(1)**. Impermeable rock is more effective as it is stronger, and better able to support the weight of the dam **(1)**. Forestry would remove some of the available precipitation through interception, reducing the amount of water available for storage **(1)**. Mountainous areas receive more rainfall and snowmelt in the spring, which can keep the reservoirs full **(1)**.

Site C has a very small catchment area with few tributaries, so less water would be available for storage **(1)**. It has impermeable rock, so it is suitable for taking the weight of the dam as well as reducing seepage **(1)**. It is close to an urban area, so the dam would control flooding and ensure a water supply/power **(1)**.   **5 marks**

b) **Hint:** You should refer to a case study you have studied, naming particular examples. You must discuss positive and negative effects. Marks will be awarded for environmental effects so avoid discussing social and economic effects unless they are linked to the environment.

If Colorado River chosen:

The creation of reservoirs encourages wildlife into an area; for example, more than 250 species of birds have been counted in the Lake Mead area, increasing the biodiversity of the region. The original wildlife in the area has been forced to move, however, as their habitats have been destroyed by the reservoirs; for example, there are no longer beavers in Tucson **(2)**. The natural landscape has been destroyed by the building of dams and the flooding of the land by the reservoirs **(1)**. In some areas the level of the reservoirs is so high that natural structures are being destroyed; for example, the Rainbow Bridge is being slowly dissolved by the waters of Lake Powell **(1)**. However, some people believe that reservoirs and dams improve the scenery, as well as supplying the area with moisture, as the amount of water infiltrating the ground is increased as a result of storage in reservoirs **(1)**. The Glen Canyon Dam is a major source of hydroelectricity, a renewable energy source that does not contribute to global warming **(1)**. When the Glen Canyon Dam was completed, the free flow of the Colorado River was hampered. Sediments travelling along with the river were blocked by the dam, causing a decline in the organic material travelling down the river, reducing the water quality and affecting the aquatic life. The river is practically devoid of nutrients downstream of the Glen Canyon Dam **(1)**. Many species of fish, amphibians and insects use sediments for habitats, spawning grounds and protection; without the sediments these species are endangered. For example, the Colorado squawfish has become endangered **(1)**.   **5 marks**

8 Development and Health

a) **Hint:** You should make reference to composite indicators, as well as economic and social indicators, giving the advantages and disadvantages of each.

Problems exist when trying to evaluate the development of a country using only social indicators such as literacy rates, because they are only averages across a country and are therefore likely to hide regional differences **(1)**. An individual indicator such as GNP is also an average, so may be easily skewed by a few very wealthy families, masking extreme poverty for the majority of the population **(1)**. A single economic indicator is inaccurate as it does not show the wealth of a country and it does not show data on how well-educated people are or how good their diet is **(1)**. Single economic indicators do not take into account differences between urban and rural areas, for example in Brazil, between poor favelas and richer inner cities **(1)**. PQLI combines a range of both social and economic indicators to give a more accurate representation of the overall quality of life of citizens in a particular country, and therefore how developed it is **(1)**. PQLI provides a much more accurate assessment of the level of development of any given country, so it also allows for comparisons of development levels between countries **(1)**.   **4 marks**

b) **Hint:** Avoid simple description. You must explain each point you make. Always try to give examples to illustrate your answer.

Countries with extreme climates, for example many countries in the Sahel region of Africa, suffer from drought and find it hard to develop as it is difficult to produce enough food to feed their populations **(1)**. This leads to malnutrition and a reduced capacity to work or create income, which results in money being borrowed from developed countries and hence debt **(1)**. It is difficult to farm, travel and earn a living in mountainous countries such as Nepal, which hampers development **(1)**. Areas likely to be hit by floods, hurricanes, volcanic eruptions or earthquakes tend to remain less developed as buildings, farming and industry could be destroyed at any time; it would cost a lot of money to replace them so the area is less attractive for foreign investors **(1)**. Developing countries tend to have more jobs in the primary sector, with low levels of trade, and are often under the influence of multinational companies. The resulting profits tend to go abroad rather than being reinvested in the country **(1)**. Areas lacking in mineral resources (for example coal, diamonds, oil) will remain less developed; minerals such as oil are in great demand and can be sold for a huge profit, giving the country a high GDP and money to invest in development, for example Kuwait **(1)**. Countries with a poor education system have many low-skilled workers and are unable to attract foreign investment **(1)**. Many developing countries have high population growth; this generally limits development as resources such as food, space and water have to be spread more thinly; there may not be enough jobs, houses, schools or health clinics to serve the population **(1)**.   **6 marks**

9 Global Climate Change

a) **Hint:** Read the question carefully. You need only give answers for physical environment causes. Avoid talking about human environment causes as this will get you no marks. Do not list the causes, as this will get you few, if any, marks. You need to show the relationship between the cause and how it affects climate change.

Global mean temperatures can be raised by peaks of sunspot activity, which follow an eleven-year cycle **(1)**. Volcanic eruptions can release huge amounts of ash into the atmosphere, which reduces the amount of solar energy reaching the Earth. This causes the Earth to become cooler for a period of time **(1)**; for example, the eruption of Krakatoa in 1883 caused a 'year without summer' due to the size and violence of the eruption **(1)**. Changes in the tilt of the Earth towards or away from the Sun can affect the amount of insolation that the Earth receives. The greater the tilt of the Earth towards the Sun, the closer some areas are to the Sun and so the greater energy they receive **(1)**. The Earth rotates around the Sun in an elliptical orbit, therefore at certain times the Earth is much closer to the Sun and receives more energy. These variations in the Earth's orbit around the Sun are called Milankovitch cycles **(1)**. Melting ice caps release additional fresh water, leading to changes in oceanic circulation **(1)**.   **4 marks**

b)   **Hint:** Avoid a list of effects or simple descriptive points. You should give advantages and disadvantages as well as referring to specific examples in your answer.

Sea levels are rising due to the increase in temperature; this causes the water to expand and is increased by the melting of the ice caps **(1)**. This threatens low-lying land and could cause the loss of farmland and the livelihoods of 80 million people across the globe, including the Shetland Islands (Scotland), Bangladesh and Japan, who might be forced to relocate **(1)**. Hurricanes and other storms are likely to become stronger and more frequent as global warming takes effect, resulting in the destruction of property and lives **(1)**. Precipitation has increased across the globe on average leading to flooding, such as in the Somerset Levels in England, and may continue to rise **(1)**. While some areas will experience more rainfall, for example Sweden, others could become drier, such as the Great Plains in America **(1)**. Floods and droughts will become more common; in Ethiopia for example, where droughts are already common, rainfall could decline by 10 per cent over the next 50 years, leading to increased desertification **(1)**. Tropical diseases such as yellow fever could spread into other areas as warmer areas expand, with up to 40 million more people in Africa being exposed to the risk of malaria **(1)**. Some areas could have a longer growing season, improving the food supply as well as increasing the variety of crops which can be grown **(1)**.   **6 marks**

10   Trade, Aid and Geopolitics

a)   **Hint:** Avoid describing the trend in commodity prices. You need to explain the impact it has on the people/country in the developing world. Using specific examples in your answer should improve your mark.

Developing countries mostly trade and export raw or partially processed goods; any variation in the prices obtained from them have an important impact on the economies and living standards of those countries **(1)**. Commodity price instability has a negative impact on economic growth, a country's financial resources, and income distribution, and may lead to increased poverty; many countries, especially in Africa, derive more than 90 per cent of their export earnings from commodities **(1)**. World commodity prices are very unstable, driven by changes in global demand and supply; developing countries are particularly affected by these changes, which can result in increased poverty and reduced public funding for health and education **(1)**. Less money coming in means that many children are forced to work instead of going to school; this leads to an illiterate population that is unable to access well-paid employment and a poorer quality of life for these people **(1)**. The lack of well-paid jobs means that many people live in shanty towns with little access to clean water, electricity or sanitation **(1)**; this enables diseases such as cholera to spread rapidly and lowers the life expectancy for people living there **(1)**. **4 marks**

b) **Hint:** Putting detail into your answer will gain you marks, so avoid simple description.

Fair trade guarantees a fair price for produce that always covers the cost of production regardless of the market price **(1)**. This allows farmers benefiting from fair trade to have security for the future and to make plans to improve their quality of life **(1)**. In normal trade there are many links between the producer and the seller, resulting in the farmer losing money; the middle men are removed in fair trade, ensuring a better return for the farmer **(1)**. Fair trade encourages farmers to look after the environment and to produce crops in a sustainable manner, protecting the land for future generations **(1)**. Fair trade also ensures that there are no child workers, so that children get the chance to attend school and improve their opportunities for the future **(1)**. As well as individual farmers, fair trade benefits entire communities with improvement payments to villages that supply fair trade coffee beans. This allows new schools and health centres to be built and staffed that would otherwise not have existed **(1)**. **6 marks**

11 Energy

a) **Hint:** Only discuss non-renewable sources of power. Do not describe the different types. You need to evaluate both good and bad points. You can evaluate them individually or collectively.

Fossil fuels, such as coal, oil and gas, are abundant in many countries throughout the world, for example Australia, which means they are a relatively cheap fuel and readily available **(1)**. Very large amounts of electricity can be generated from fossil fuels and they can also be moved to where power is being generated relatively easily, making them cost-effective and easier to use **(1)**. However, once sources of non-renewable energy are gone they cannot be replaced or renewed, so they are not a viable long-term solution for energy use **(1)**. The mining of non-renewable energy sources and the by-products they leave behind causes damage to the environment **(1)**. Fossil fuels contribute to global warming: greenhouse gases are emitted when fossil fuels burn, nitrous oxides cause photochemical pollution and sulphur dioxide creates acid rain **(1)**. The prices of non-renewable fuels such as oil are subject to fluctuation due to wars and other international differences; this can affect economies throughout the world **(1)**. **5 marks**

b) **Hint:** In this question you should try to use facts from the graph. You should give reasons for the increase or decrease in energy demand.

The population of countries like India and China continues to grow, as does their standard of living. Electricity for lighting and appliances such as televisions, washing machines and air conditioning will all cause energy use to increase **(1)**. China's industries continue to grow, with most growth centred on manufacturing industries, which use up vast amounts of power. In developed countries there is now an emphasis on service and quaternary industries, which use much less power **(1)**. In a global economy many of the manufactured products are sold to developed countries and therefore need to be transported around the world – using energy **(1)**. Car-ownership rates increase as people in developing countries become more prosperous, resulting in greater energy consumption **(1)**. In developed countries the population growth rates are more stable, or even falling, so there is no great increase in demand for energy **(1)**. New products and technologies are also increasingly energy efficient, which keeps energy consumption steadier in developed countries **(1)**.   **5 marks**

Section 4: Application of Geographical Skills

12 **Hint:** This scenario question is designed to examine your geographical skills, including interpreting an Ordnance Survey map, using six-figure grid references and understanding/using scale, direction and distance. You should also be able to extract and interpret information from a variety of graphs and charts. In this question you will be able to demonstrate to the examiner the geographical skills you have learned and developed throughout your Higher course. You should use/evaluate the information you have been given to make judgements and back up your answer with map evidence and information from the diagrams. This question is worth 10 marks.

On the Ordnance Survey map and Diagram Q12C it can be seen that the turbines will be spread out over a large area to the west of Stornoway, so far enough away from the town to cause little impact from the noise of the turbines **(1)**, for example at 348318 the furthest turbines are about five miles distant **(1)**. However, Diagram Q12D shows that the turbines are tall and many are strung out along the A859. This is the main route into Stornoway, so the turbines will have a negative impact on the view **(1)**, and since this area attracts tourists for its beauty and tranquillity the visual and noise pollution caused by the turbines could deter tourists from coming to the area, adversely affecting the local tourist economy **(1)**. Charlie Macleod in Diagram Q12D says video evidence proves that wind turbines are noisy and visually unattractive and since the ones being proposed for Stornoway are much taller and more powerful than those in the videos, the overall impact will actually be worse, thus adversely affecting the local population **(1)**. However, the Ordnance Survey map shows this is a remote area with only a small population, mainly located in Stornoway, with the only other settlement being a string of dwellings spread along the A859 at grid reference 3129, so the wind farm will affect only a small number of people **(1)**.

As shown in Diagram Q12A, the wind farm needs an average wind speed of at least 11 miles per hour to be effective. Diagram Q12A shows that for 10 months of the year, from August through to May, the wind speed meets this condition **(1)**. In the winter months of November, December, January and February the wind speed on average is much higher, reaching speeds of up to 18 miles per hour. This can be a problem because if the wind speed is too high then the turbines might need to be turned off for safety reasons, thus producing no electricity **(1)**. The summer months of June and July are also a problem as the average wind speed is only 10 miles per hour, which is below the speed needed, so no power can be produced **(1)**.

The Ordnance Survey map shows areas of forestry, for example at 340305. Parts of the wind farm will be built in this area so trees will need to be removed, destroying the natural woodland as well as the local animal habitat, which could threaten their survival **(1)**. Fewer trees could result in the decline of carbon storage, as trees take in carbon dioxide and give out oxygen, as well as leading to increased carbon storage in the atmosphere **(1)**.

The turbines themselves can be a danger to the bird population, including species like the Golden Eagle, as birds sometimes fly into them **(1)**. However, as shown in Diagram Q12B, the Royal Society for the Protection of Birds surprisingly is not totally opposed to the wind farm. While it can and does object to some wind farms, if the developer is prepared to follow certain guidelines it will support the project, for example ensuring the turbines are not placed directly in bird migration routes, thus reducing the impact on the local bird population **(1)**.

In Diagram Q12D Eilidh McKinnon feels the development should not go ahead, as digging up the moorland to place the turbines will destroy the traditional way of life of people like her. As a crofter, she uses the moor for sheep grazing and looks after the land in a sympathetic manner; she feels the money offered by the developer does not compensate for the destruction of the natural environment **(1)**. However, Angus Campbell takes the opposite view. The area has very few sources of employment and this development is providing jobs as well as supporting the local economy, as workers will spend money in the local shops, etc., so the project should go ahead **(1)**. The local crofters would actually benefit from the development as they would receive payments from the developer for renting out their land to allow the turbines to be placed there, thus improving their standard of living **(1)**. Increase in employment also means increased taxes getting paid to the government, improving the economy of the whole of Scotland **(1)**. Stornoway Wind, the developers of the project, obviously want the project to go ahead as they would make a profit **(1)**.

Lastly, wind power is green energy so it is good for the planet and reduces global warming **(1)**. It reduces the need for energy being produced from fossil fuels, thus reducing the carbon footprint **(1)** as well as helping towards Scotland's carbon reduction target of 80 per cent by 2050, as shown in Diagram Q12E **(1)**.

Looking at all the evidence, I feel this project should go ahead. I think the disadvantages like the noise and visual pollution and loss of some habitat are well offset by the financial benefits and the reduction in the carbon footprint **(1)**.